A CELEBRATION FOR EDITH SITWELL
ON THE OCCASION OF HER VISIT
TO THE UNITED STATES

Direction

A series of paper bound books published by New Directions.

Individual numbers are priced at $1.50 each. It is possible, however, to subscribe for advance issues at the rate of 4 numbers for $2. Payment should be sent with orders to New Directions, Norfolk, Connecticut.

A Celebration For
EDITH SITWELL

edited by JOSE GARCIA VILLA

Direction

SEVEN

PRINTED BY DUDLEY KIMBALL
AT THE BLUE RIDGE MOUNTAIN PRESS
PARSIPPANY, NEW JERSEY

CONTENTS

A REMINISCENCE

Sir Osbert Sitwell

In this number of *Direction* devoted to celebrating the work of my sister, I have decided to say nothing of her poems, about which others can write. Instead, I wish to rescue an episode from her childhood and record it, because it may provide a clue, self-confessed, to the secret of her subsequent achievement. Since it occurred about the time I was born, or a few months later, it is not a personal memory: but, instead, a reconstruction, though to me it almost ranks as a memory, so well can I recall the few people who figure on this particular stage, the scene itself, and the background, and so often did I, long ago, hear the incident mentioned in the various tones of regret, reprobation and shame reserved for it. The childish lack of modesty, the childish directness and certainty it exemplified, made a mark at the time, and subsequently left a scar on the family consciousness.

When I first remember her, my sister was recognisable as a youthful version of what she is now, the same carriage, long limbs, and Byzantine or Sienese profile. But at the time of which I am writing, only a year or two earlier, she was only just emerging from babyhood, and several photographs remain to testify to an almost unidentifiably different appearance; then she was a sturdy, indeed—let us be frank—, a fat child. She was dressed in dark green serge, with gaiters, and wore a fur cap, her hair was golden and curled at the side of a full-moon face. Only the deep-set, hooded, tragic eyes of the poet she was to become spoke

7

out from this mask of childhood, telling us of her future and of the world's; for the eyes seemed to contemplate with full consciousness and with a brooding compassion the forces at work to end the gay and glittering surfaces around us, and those who walked across them: but the green glance of these grey-blue eyes was directed within, too, towards the infinity of the human soul, as well as towards the exterior aspect.

There was no hint of the windy, desolate spaces of the future, but perhaps she already saw them in the room at which we are looking, the large drawing-room on the first floor, furnished in elegant, mandarin taste, with Chippendale chairs and cabinets. Outside the windows, wide open—for it is a warm seaside day of early spring—shows a floor of green tree-tops, cut flat, as though to provide a stage for the furious winds to dance when the winter comes, and, beyond, a vast expanse of light blue sea merging into the light blue sky that covers us, covers all. Somewhere, far away, distinctly to be heard in the smiling town, so neat and clearly defined in its empty, causeless gaiety that alternates with an emptier, causeless depression, a hurdy-gurdy was playing. In the room, my mother was sitting in the light sunshine and shadows, and a figure was standing by the central windows; Rita, a friend of hers who had come to stay, not beautiful, like my mother, but a more fashionable variation we should think her now, if we could see her, of a young woman painted by Seurat or Renoir—though of course no influence from these painters existed in her, but on the contrary, she was merely part of the vast material the spirit of the times provided for those artists. She was dressed in light colours and her waist was famous for its slenderness; as she stood there, the light outlining her contours, she seemed to possess the exaggerated elegance of a Cretan Priestess-Acrobat. My mother was wearing clothes of a different kind, of a more sporting cut, for she always, if possible, marred in the day time the perfection of her Italian looks with this hard, inappropriate, yet characteristic style. In opposition to it, however, she wore a large bunch of tuberoses. The room was full of huge vases of flowers, and my father, who stood in the background, was lifting

8

them up with a somewhat furtive air to see if the water had run down the sides to leave rings of damp on the polished tops of tables and cabinets. He did not seem to pay much attention to what was in progress in the room or to what was said.

My mother rang the bell and told the footman to send for Davies and Miss Edith. She did not want to see her, for the child, whom sometimes she really hated, always filled her with fear: for the little creature possessed a striking personal dignity, she used words occasionally, of which she could hardly at her age —five—comprehend the meaning, and in general seemed disagreeably unlike the children of friends and relations. Her way of seeing things was surprising, and unsuitable, as my father also thought, to the charm that should invest childhood for the parents with a sticky but romantic gloss. Her truthfulness, in particular, though truthful, was objectionably unlike the truth of other children and she showed a love of music which seemed to him excessive and exaggerated . . . But Rita, who had just arrived, liked the child and wanted to see her; so my father and mother both had to pretend to want to see her too.

After a moment or two the door opened and Davies the nurse, in her black bonnet and grey alpaca coat and skirt, ushered the little girl in and stood by the door, a kindly, impassive figure with eyes full of the devotion she felt for her charge, and of the kindly bewilderment that was habitual to her expression. The child advanced into the middle of the room, and seemed to fill it with her personality, so that it even conquered the strong, individual atmosphere that my mother and father imparted.

"Well, little E., do you remember me?" the guest enquired . . .

The child regarded her for a moment with large, melancholy eyes and then, after a period of reflection, spoke firmly the monosyllable "No!"

This was a bad beginning. My mother laughed uneasily; my father put down another vase and said, "The memory of children is often curiously uneven." . . .

Worse was to come. Rita shifted the conversational ground, so as to disguise her smiling dismay. She looked at the little girl

9

standing alone, with a singular isolation in the sunlight, splintered and dappled by the shimmering sea and the flecking, fleecy clouds, and spoke again inclining kindly, as much as her figure allowed, towards the child.

"And what are you going to be when you grow up?"

This time the reply came without any pause for reflection, straight, clear, final.

"A genius!"

My mother blushed for the shame she felt. My father cleared his throat while his eyes avoided those of the other two grown-ups. The child was withdrawn from circulation, but the incident rankled and was often referred to as an example to be avoided. It was never, I believe spoken of outside the walls until now.

IMAGES IN THE POETIC WORLD OF EDITH SITWELL

Stephen Spender

A recent adverse critic of Miss Sitwell's poems quotes Gerard Manley Hopkins catechizing Browning for monstrousness in his use of imagery. Hopkins held "that Browning was 'not really a poet, that he has all the gifts but the one needful and the pearls without the string; rather, one should say raw nuggets and rough diamonds.' His turning of concave into convex" (when he compared heaven in *Instans Tyrranus* to a shield protecting the just man from tyrants) "was a 'frigidity,' an 'untruth to nature'."

Emboldened by the example of Hopkins, Mr. Geoffrey Grigson quotes examples of "monstrosities," "untruths to nature," in the recent poems of Edith Sitwell. For example,

> . . . *bird-blood leaps within our veins*
> *And is changed to emeralds like the sap in the grass.*
>
> *And you are the sound of the growth of spring in the*
> *heart's deep core.*
>
> *And I would that each hair on my head was an angel*
> *O my red Adam.*
>
> *O heed him not, my dew with golden feet*
> *Flying from me.*

And so on and so on. The list could be added to indefinitely until it includes practically everything that Miss Sitwell has written: because this is her way of writing, and if one can criticize it for not being close to nature then criticism is easy game, and there is little more to be said.

11

Mr. Grigson, of course, quotes Dryden, to show the kind of consistent parallel development of the interior movement of poetry with the external organic movement of nature, he thinks a poem should contain.

This kind of criticism starts off with an assumption which —despite Hopkins on Browning—should be the conclusion rather than the beginning of an argument. One has only to glance at Shakespeare and take a by no means extreme example from *Hamlet*. One line will do:

> *To crook the pregnant hinges of the knee.*

Enough to point out that Dryden would not have written this line and that it is difficult to see how Hopkins could have approved of it. When we come to recent poetry, the thought of the Romantics, of Rimbaud, of the Symbolists, the Imagists and the Surrealists should give us pause before we decide that imagery must be true to nature. On the face of it, such an assumption looks like a prejudice which may be held with great fervour by those who prefer one kind of poetry to another. But there is no basis on which the "nature" school can argue that the inventors of an artificial type of imagery do not write poetry.

It is interesting, though, to approach Miss Sitwell's poetry from the side of her imagery. For it is in the development of her imagery that her growth as a poet and as a human being living a spiritual life in her poetry are most apparent. And it is in a study of her imagery that one has the firmest grasp of the experience of life that her poetry does express. Her imagery may not be photographically representative of nature, but it is true to a very real experience.

Basically, Miss Sitwell's imagery is of a kind which one must call artificial. But the development of her poetry has been to infuse ever more observation of society and even of nature, more emotion, more experience into this imagery, which still has a hard clear quality like transparent stone. It is exactly this forcing, as it were, of blood into stone which makes her later poetry so remarkable.

In the early poems, the artificiality is so striking, that in a

12

characteristic passage such as the following, without having to be Mr. Grigson one can see that this is not "like nature":—

> At Easter when red lacquer buds sound far slow
> Quarter-tones for the old dead Mikado,
> Through avenues of lime-trees, where the wind
> Sounds like a chapeau chinois, shrill, unkind,—
> The Dowager Queen, a curling Korin wave
> That flows for ever past a coral cave,
> With Dido, Queen of Carthage, slowly drives
> (Her griffin dog that has a thousand lives)
> Upon the flat-pearled and fantastic shore
> Where curled and turbanned waves sigh "Nevermore,"
> And she is sunk beneath a clear still lake
> Of sleep,—so frail with age she cannot wake. . . .

This is a world of artifice kept at a certain distance from nature—a distance which is perhaps measured and indicated by the phrase "red lacquer buds" which is just like and just unlike enough to make one realize that Miss Sitwell's world is real and unreal at the same time. One steps backwards and forwards from the almost-real, the almost-true, to the fantastic and completely artificial. This happens not only on the plane of observation but also on that of feeling. The feelings most often provoked by these early poems are enchantment, humour and pity. The writing is at once sophisticated and very simple, with a simplicity bordering at times almost on the primitive and the childish.

I first read these early poems of Miss Sitwell when I was sixteen. At this time I was enchanted by them and my own early efforts were often their imitators. Later I valued them for lines which still seem to me of a ravishing beauty:—

> The coral-cold snow seemed the Parthenon . . .
> The birds, strange flashing glints of another life,
> Peck at the fruits of summer, that too soon
> Will fade into a little gilded dust.
> For us he wandered over each old lie,
> Changing the flowering hawthorn, full of bees,
> Into the silver helm of Hercules. . . .

13

Turning back to these poems again, I am amazed at the consistency of quality with which they are imagined. They create pictures, hard, angular, toy-like, brightly coloured and vividly seen, extremely self-contained, which are unlike any other poetry. There persists through them the personality of the poet which one gets to know well, though one seems to know it in an external way, much as one knows her world from the outside. One knows when she laughs, when she is mercilessly satiric and when she melts with pity, but one does not feel oneself in contact with the very springs of her emotion.

It appears to me that the first quality which one requires of poetry is that it should create. If a poet even creates a few images, a few haunting lines, that is already something. Next one asks that creativeness should be sustained and that there should be a consistency of mood and purpose within a poem, however violent the superficial changes of manner. A poem which has been completely created in detail and as a whole, exists in the mind of the reader as a kind of object, a single impression, like any other remembered experience. And as with other experiences one compares poems and finds that they have qualities which differ from each other, and that some make a profounder impression than others. All the same, once a poem has been accepted as a definite experience, only prejudice can dismiss it by inventing some reason for refusing to examine it seriously.

Miss Sitwell's early poems seem to me, firstly, definitely to be works of art which have been fully created. On the other hand those universal qualities do not go into them which make one turn to them constantly as illuminations which seem to have a living relationship to all the most vital passages of one's life. In a good sense, they are "fashionable," beautifully made and highly idiosyncratic works which one delights in in certain moods but which one does not always want. They are likely, with much other poetry, to go out of fashion and then to be rediscovered again.

The great difference between the early and the later poetry is that in the later poems, the whole inner personality of the poet and a lifetime of experience, have entered. But between the early

14

and the late work, there is a bridge, supplied by the astonishing poem called "Gold Coast Customs" (A poem, by the way, greatly admired by W. B. Yeats, partly perhaps because he also was a poet of fantasy and artifice).

"Gold Coast Customs" is a poem in which the ceremonies of a tribe of the Ashantees are juxtaposed with a picture of fashionable party life in civilized countries. It is a commonplace, of course, that all customs are barbaric. But the intensity of vision which is haunted by the insistent connection between the civilized and the barbaric is very rare. For, essentially, to see this connection of the pursuits of a civilization which one is taught to regard as civilised with a so-called barbarous civilization, is essentially to see the mocking shape of barbarity and death under all the pretences and all the aims of all existence, whether in Europe or in Africa.

In "Gold Coast Customs," Miss Sitwell's artificiality is used to new purpose, with astonishing effect. It achieves the synthesis which can place one kind of civilization beside another. The barbaric and the civilized both become slightly unreal within the medium of her manner, and the result is that they become identical. The artifice of "Gold Coast Customs" throws that of the early poems into a new light. One begins to see the sense of artificiality not as something superficially imposed on the poet's experience but as part of her experience of life itself. She is obsessed by the feeling that human behavior is artificial. It is this which gives her fantastic approach to reality its consistency, which is an inner consistency of her whole personality.

In her later work there is a wholeness due partly to the development of her own personality, partly to a deepening of sympathy with the suffering of other people during the recent years of anguish and war. Her poems have at the same time broadened far beyond any personal idiosyncrasies and become more deeply personal. "Serenade: Any Man to Any Woman" begins

> Dark angel, who are clear and straight
> As cannon shining in the air,
> Your blackness doth invade my mind

15

> *And thunderous as the armoured wind*
> *That rained on Europe is your hair. . . .*

The invasion of France has already become absorbed into this poet's strange world: and perhaps only a world as personal as Miss Sitwell's is capable of absorbing so directly, and then recreating, such an immediate and violent experience.

Two impressions predominate in her mature later work. One is the music, and the other the imagery. The music is, as it were, a horizontal movement which in its long, measured beat has a certain appeal also to the eye. The imagery gives a sense of verticality. It suggests upright figures, the sun in the height of the heavens, the pillar of fire, trees, etc. There is more to it, though, than this. There is also a prostrate imagery of death, earth enclosing bodies in its dust, kings who have died long ago. Miss Sitwell's extraordinary control of her medium is due to her power of keeping impressions separated from each other. She is like a painter who uses very simple colours, but who makes them all glow and who gives them a structural purpose: or, again, she is like a composer who is extremely conscious of the use of intervals and of notes widely separated from each other. This effect of the separation of music from imagery and of image from image can only be attained by the simplest means used with the greatest intensity and clarity of purpose. By invoking the same images again and again, by using very often the same rhymes, Miss Sitwell makes us throughly acquainted with the notes of her instrument, on which she produces her prodigious hymns.

> *We are the darkness in the heat of the day,*
> *The rootless flowers in the air, the coolness: we are*
> > *the water*
> *Lying upon the leaves before Death, our sun,*
> *And its vast heat has drunken us . . . Beauty's*
> > *daughter*
> *The heart of the rose and we are one.*

Here one has the long, horizontal, measured beat, manipulated with faint disturbance—the disturbance of a comma or of three full-stops—to indicate the restlessness above the calm of a summer evening. The imagery itself all suggests things standing or things prostrate, the rootless flowers, the sun.

Although it is easy enough to describe Miss Sitwell's effects, it is not easy to say why they are successful. The subject matter is very general, dealing with death, love and life in their most universal aspects. And the epithets are very simple: the sun, the rose, water, gold, are invoked again and again. Nevertheless, these generalized ideas and simple images exist within a world which remains always entirely Miss Sitwell's own. They are convincing because the whole of her personality is projected into her poetry, and her mature personality brings with it the preoccupations of Europe at this time. Miss Sitwell exists in her poetry as Lorca exists in his ballads, and as Van Gogh in his painting and his letters. The light, the ripeness, the death and the anguish of these later poems, are as accurate a picture as we have of an interior life of the spirit in our time. This poetry comes from a great isolation allied to a widening sympathy: such an isolation as we remark in the later work of Yeats and of T. S. Eliot, which is perhaps the only way for the poet in our time.

A poet's use of imagery can only be criticized in the light of his artistic purpose: and one can understand this not by quoting single lines out of their context, but by considering the use of imagery in an entire poem. Here, then, let us consider a poem entitled "Anne Boleyn's Song."

'After the terrible rain, the Annunciation'—
The bird-blood in the veins that has changed to emeralds
Answered the bird-call . . .
In the neoteric Spring the winter coldness
Will be forgotten
As I forget the coldness of my last lover,

The great grey King
Who lies upon my breast
And rules the bird-blood in my veins that shrieked with
    laughter
—A sound like fear—

When my step light and high
Spurned my sun down from the sky
In my heedless headless dance—
O many a year ago, my dear,
My living lass!

In the nights of Spring, the bird, the Angel of the
    Annunciation.
Broods over his heaven of wings and of green wild-fire
That each in its own world, each in its egg
Like Fate is lying.

He sang to my blood, as Henry, my first King,
My terrible sun
Came like the Ethos of Spring, the first green streak,
And to me cried,
'Your veins are the branches where the first blossom begins
After the winter rains—
Your eyes are black and deep
As the prenatal sleep
And your arms and your breasts are my Rivers of Life
While a new world grows in your side.'
Men said I was the primal Fall,
That I gave him the world of Spring and of youth like an
    apple
And the orchards' emerald lore—
And sin lay at the core.

But Henry thought me winter-cold
When to leave his love I turned from him as the world
Turns from the sun . . . and then the world grew old—
But I who grew in the heart as the bird-song
Grows in the heart of Spring . . . I, terrible Angel
Of the emeralds in the blood of man and tree,
How could I know how cold the nights of Spring would be.

When my grey glittering King—
Old amorous Death grew acclimatized to my coldness:
His age sleeps on my breast,

18

My veins, like branches where the first peach-blossom
Trembles, bring the Spring's warmth to his greyness.

This poem is an excellent example of the quality which I
have called stone-like, made transparent with a passion as of light
shining through it. The inner theme of Miss Sitwell's later poems
is often transformation—the transformation of life into death, of
warmth into coldness, of love into hatred. This sense of transformation is something which takes place within the images
themselves. One must judge these images not as being de-
rived from natural processes but from unnatural ones—chemical
changes of one substance into another, identification of opposites
one with the other. There is a tendency in this poem to trans-
form human feeling into something at first inhuman and then
altogether cold and mineral. The blood of the queen first
suggests bird-blood and then emeralds. This process of metamorphosis is interwoven with the associations of Spring, birds in
branches and green leaves. The polar opposites, heat and cold,
sun and earth, life and death dominate the poem. One is reminded of some lines of Yeats which describe the experience of
all these poems:—

> *Once out of nature I shall never take*
> *My bodily form of any natural thing,*
> *But such a form as Grecian goldsmiths make*
> *Of hammered gold and gold enamelling*
> *To keep a drowsy Emperor awake;*
> *Or set upon a golden bough to sing*
> *To lords and ladies of Byzantium*
> *Of what is past, or passing, or to come.*

THE WAR POETRY OF EDITH SITWELL

Maurice Bowra

With the publication of *Street Songs* in 1942 and *Green Song* in 1944, Miss Edith Sitwell has not only won an almost unique place for herself among the poets of this war but abundantly ful-filled the highest hopes which her admirers have had of her. This great flowering of her genius is her reward for years of devoted and patient labour at her art. From her first beginnings she possessed an instinctive sense for the true essence of poetry and a sensibility so fine and delicate that it can detect all the subtle echoes and associations which float round the sounds of human speech. She set herself a hard task when she made up her mind to restore to English poetry the richness of texture which had been largely lost in the Edwardian and Georgian epochs. For this reason much of her early work was experimental. She experimented with rhythms, with the values of vowels and consonants, with new kinds of imagery and with unaccustomed themes. Of this preparatory work, in many ways so brilliant and so fascinating, she is herself a stern critic. When she published her *Collected Poems* in 1930, she omitted many pieces that others would wish to be included. But she had her own good reasons. She was content only with her best work; the rest was experimental and must be excluded. Yet even in this remarkable volume she had not found the full range of her gifts. Though "The Sleeping Beauty" showed of what enchanting fancy and haunting melody she was capable and "Gold Coast Customs" showed what tragic power and prophetic

20

fury were hers, it was not until the Second World War that she fused all her different gifts into a single kind of poetry and combined in noble harmony her delicate fancy, her uncommon visual sense, her tender sympathy, her heroic courage in the face of a shattered world and her deep religious trust in the ultimate goodness of life.

In these two latest volumes Miss Sitwell has brought her technique to perfection. Her verse moves with unfailing ease and flexibility. She has so mastered its intricacies that it seems to respond without effort to any demands that her changing moods may make of it, to be equally effective in long, rolling lines or in the brief tune of a song. Her rhymes come so easily that we hardly notice them, though they make their essential contribution to the final, musical result. Her vocabulary, which looks so unpretentious, has been purified and polished by long, discriminating selection. When she permits herself an unusual word, such as 'pyromaniacs' or 'ombrelle,' it comes with all the greater effect because of the simplicity of its surroundings. But the central triumph of this art is that Miss Sitwell has succeeded in her first aim of restoring its texture to poetry. Her work is first and always poetry and makes its chief appeal to the imagination through the ear and the inner eye. There is no padding, no hackneyed phraseology, no attempt to cover imprecision of thought or feeling by vague, vast words, no lapse into unimaginative flatness or lifeless echoes from other poets. The subtly varying rhythms respond with exquisite tact to the movements of the poet's sensibility. Each word is chosen with a keen appreciation of its sound-values. It would be pleasant to dilate on almost any verse in this poetry and to show what consummate skill has gone to its creation. An example, taken at random, must suffice:

> And with them come gaps into listening darkness:
> The Gun-men, the molochs, the matadors, man-eaters,
> Hiding in islands of loneliness, each one
> Infections of hatred, and greed-plague, and fear.

The half-concealed alliterations, the occasional monosyllables, like 'gaps' and 'fear,' placed with so powerful an emphasis, the grating sound of such words as 'molochs' and 'greed-plague,' the rise of the whole verse to a crisis of emotion, the imaginative precision with which the different powers of destruction are chosen and named, all these are the fruits of a technique so accomplished that it never asserts itself or attracts our attention. The result, clean and direct and powerful, shows no traces of its workshop and merely makes us feel how impressively and nobly Miss Sitwell writes.

This perfected technique is used to convey experiences of tragic grandeur and intensity. Miss Sitwell is a seer, a prophetess. Just as in "Gold Coast Customs" she denounced the hideous emptiness and bestiality of modern life, so now she sees with anguish and torment the devastation wrought by the war. Though the years have brought her patience and detachment, and though she no longer feels herself an active figure on the human stage, she responds with all the warmth of her compassionate heart to the carnage and desolation round her and shows what they mean to her, what wounds they have dealt to her and with what vision and courage she has sought an answer to the ugly questions which they raise. In "Green Flows the River of Lethe-O" she tells of the spiritual journey on which she has gone. Once she tried to stand apart from the empty frivolities of the world, but something inside her took control and turned her to another road:

> I was Annihilation
> Yet white as the Dead Sea, white as the Cities of the Plains.
> For I listened to the noontide and my veins
> That threatened thunder and the heart of roses.
> I went the way I would—
> But long is the terrible Street of the Blood
> That had once seemed only part of the summer redness:
> It stretches for ever, and there is no turning
> But only fire, annihilation, burning.

It is of this 'Street of the Blood' that Miss Sitwell now writes. Blood is her symbol for life, for all that beats in the heart and flows in the veins, that stirs emotions and affections and brings men closer to one another from their separate solitudes. This

22

blood, spilt so wantonly, becomes a symbol of all that happens to mankind in war, of the sacrifices and the redemption, the penalties and the consolations which rise from the madness of mutual destruction. The seer who tried to stand outside life has been dragged inexorably into it and found herself forced to share in the common human lot. This experience has been an inestimable gain to her. Her natural sympathies have found a full scope for their exercise; her creative gifts have been unified in a new strength and humanity and grandeur.

While Miss Sitwell faces her own lot and losses with an uncomplaining endurance, she is deeply outraged by the sufferings of others, especially of the young. In "Serenade" she shows with poignant insight the lot of the young lover who knows that his love is under sentence of death and can never be fulfilled. The horror of such a situation, in which every hope or pleasure is darkened by the imminence of destruction, comes out with strange magnificence in Miss Sitwell's classical octosyllabics, with their ironical echoes of passionate Elizabethan love-songs and their conclusion that the only hope of happiness for such lovers is in the grave. The lover knows that his love-making is little more than a pretence because he can never fulfil his promises or give himself up entirely to his beloved. His heart and mind must always be full of that death which hangs over him and distracts his thoughts:

> And so I love you till I die—
> (Unfaithful I, the cannon's mate):
> Forgive my love of such brief span,
> But fickle is the flesh of man,
> And death's cold puts the passion out.
>
> I'll woo you with a serenade—
> The wolfish howls the starving made;
> And lies shall be your canopy
> To shield you from the freezing sky.

Therefore the only offer that he can honestly make is

> Then die with me and be my love.

Miss Sitwell picks up words from Marlowe's "The Passionate

Shepherd to his Love" and alters them to a new and terrible significance. Just as the world at war is an inverted, topsy-turvy counterpart of what it has once been, so the modern lover's position is itself inverted. His only prospect is death, and he turns to the thought of it as once lovers turned to the thought of life. Miss Sitwell's tenderness has been deeply wounded by the barbarities of war and finds its outlet in this tragic paradox.

In "Lullaby" a similar spirit informs a vision of the levelled, devastated world that lies before modern children. To this Miss Sitwell gives a peculiar power by the myth which holds it together. She imagines that the world has returned to a state of primeval chaos. Its inhabitants are odious monsters. The bombing aeroplane has become a pterodactyl which lays steel eggs in the heart of mother-earth and then fouls its nest; the mother, symbol of the old, lost tenderness and humanity, is dead, and her place is taken by the Babioun, whose very name, taken from Ben Jonson, suggests a monstrous, hideous ape, and who becomes a foster-mother to the orphan child and sings over it a sinister, blood-curdling lullaby. The purport of this song is that the child can look for nothing in the future but a deadly, meaningless, hopeless uniformity, a world in which all distinctions have been obliterated and there is no pleasure in possession or in creation:

Hear my ragged lullaby,
Fear not living, fear not chance;
All is equal—blindness, sight,
There is no depth, there is no height;
Do, do.

The poem reflects the mood of despair which many knew in the dark early years of the war when nothing seemed likely to survive the universal destruction, and all the laborious constructions of civilisation looked as if they might perish in the night of blood. Miss Sitwell secures a specially poignant effect by using the form of a lullaby. The refrain of 'Do, do' which the Babioun sings over her foster-child recalls with ironical contrast such delicate lullabies as that of Miss Sitwell's "The Sleeping Beauty":

24

Do, do,
Princess, do,
Like a tree that drips with gold you flow
With beauty ripening very slow.

The form which was so well suited to the atmosphere of an enchanted dream is transferred with powerful effect to a hideous nightmare.

The irony of these two poems reflects the conflict which the war has created in Miss Sitwell. It is her challenge, her defiance to circumstances so malign that she cannot see an end to them, and yet she refuses to admit that they defeat her. It rises from her heroic attempt to understand a world which has apparently lost all order and reason, and it is characteristic of her that what awakes this mood is not her own plight but the plight of others. At times she passes beyond it to a more truly universal outlook, to an embracing, prophetic vision. In "The Night before Great Babylon" she gives her poetic account of a world on the edge of destruction. It begins with an evocation of lovers who need nothing but each other and find in their mutual love a complete and satisfying universe. But a wind comes and brings rain. The woman feels safe in the protection of the man, but her trust is soon shown to be an illusion:

> *But a wind came tall,*
> *The wind in his grey knight's armour,*
> *The wind in his grey night armour—*
> *And the great gold Sun was slain.*
> *'What is the wind that doth blow?*
> *It is cold, and begins to rain.'*
> *'Not only the rain is falling.'*

In this apparently simple poem, with its little story of lovers in Babylon and its compelling, evocative imagery, Miss Sitwell conveys the menace of coming doom as it strikes on the self-contained world of human affections. She attempts nothing grandiose or spectacular and relies for her main effect on the contrast between

25

two perfectly chosen events, the young woman rapt in her love and the sudden burst of wind and rain with the unnamed horror that comes with them. The last line of the poem, so simple in its presentation and so rich in imaginative suggestion, catches the moment of transition from the old secure world to the new world of unforeseen horror.

The imagery of rain is developed with enormous power in "Still Falls the Rain," which has claims to be the most profound and most moving poem yet written in English about the war. It was inspired by the air-raids of 1940, but it has nothing transitory or merely contemporary about it. It is an intense, highly imaginative and tragic poem on the sufferings of man. The rain which falls in "The Night before Great Babylon" now realises all the fears that are there held of it and becomes a real rain of destruction from the sky. Real and horrible though it is, it has a great metaphysical and symbolical significance. It is an example and a sign of the suffering which man inflicts upon himself, or rather which human depravity inflicts on the innocent human heart. The opening lines show that this new abomination is a kind of crucifixion:

> Still falls the Rain—
> Dark as the world of man, black as our loss—
> Blind as the nineteen hundred and forty nails
> Upon the Cross.

The rain falls impartially on rich, on poor, on just and unjust. All are equal beneath it. It is like the blood which flows from the wounded side of the 'Starved Man,' of the Christ who is in every man, and it comes from the wounds which mankind has dealt to itself:

> The last faint spark
> In the self-murdered heart, the wounds of the sad uncomprehending dark,
> The wounds of the baited bear,—
> The blind and weeping bear whom the keepers beat
> On his helpless flesh . . . the tears of the hunted hare.

26

Yet this suffering, so hideous and yet in some ways so inevitable and so deserved, is not hopeless or irretrievable. The falling blood is like the blood of Christ and brings redemption even to those who have inflicted the wounds. When the dawn comes,

> Then sounds the voice of One who like the heart of man
> Was once a child who among beasts has lain—
> 'Still do I love, still shed my innocent light, my Blood for
>   thee.'

So the destruction wrought by the air-raids is transformed into an example of man's wickedness and punishment and redemption. He brings his own sufferings upon himself, but through them he may be redeemed. So Miss Sitwell passes beyond the horror of the present moment to a vision of its significance in the spiritual history of man and through her compassion for him finds a ray of hope for his future.

Miss Sitwell understands the war-stricken with more than an ordinary woman's insight. In such a time there are many who feel that the struggle is too much for them and turn with longing to the thought of death. Miss Sitwell knows what they think and enters so naturally into their minds that she seems almost to identify herself with them and to speak on their behalf. From the depths of her compassionate and imaginative soul she knows what this longing for death means and why men and women have it. In "Spring" she tells how the lost and hungry cry out to death as to a fellow outcast who shares their suffering: in "Street Song" she speaks through the lips of those who wish for death because it delivers them from the apes and tigers incarnate in man:

> The holy night of conception, of rest, the consoling
> Darkness when all men are equal,—the wrong and the right
> And the rich and the poor are no longer separate nations,—
> They are brothers in night.

But though she understands this longing not only with her head but with her heart, she does not ultimately share it or admit that it is right. In "Spring" the cry of the outcasts is answered by the call of the warm earth in spring to forget their misery; in "Street

27

Song" the longing for peace and rest is resisted by the intellect
or, as Miss Sitwell calls it, the Bone, which doubts the reality of
these cries and asks if they are something else:

> Who knows if the sound was that of the dead light calling,—
> Of Caesar rolling onward his heart, that stone,
> Or the burden of Atlas falling.

It is possible that the cry is really from the depths of the human
heart as some brutal tyranny pursues its relentless way; but is no
less possible that the present agony is some little understood
process of change in the world. And when such a doubt is present,
it is wiser to wait and do nothing. So too in "One Day in Spring"
Miss Sitwell tells of a man whose wife is dead and who in his
sense of irreparable loss believes that he has ceased to love her as
he should or as he once did. For him too there is an answer. The
love which he once had is not dead. It is born again with each
year. In the end the forces of life triumph over those of death,
and the most haunting and insistent doubts are dispelled by the
warmth of the sun in the spring.

This assertion of positive values in the face of corruption and
destruction is fundamental to Miss Sitwell's poetry and gives to it
a special coherence and harmony. Against "Lullaby" and "Serenade" we must set such poems as "Harvest" and "Holiday." We
shall then see how Miss Sitwell passes through the harrowing
doubts and despairs of war to a constructive outlook. This outlook is religious. Sometimes she uses the symbols of the Christian
faith, in the Crucified whose wounds are on every human hand,
in the Holy Ghost who speaks at night 'in the whispering leaves,'
in the angels who sing through the earth. But behind this there
is something that is not narrowly or specifically Christian, unless
it be a kind of Christian pantheism. For Miss Sitwell the earth
is more than the garment of God; it is a manifestation of God
himself. In the rebirth of natural forces and the comfort and
strength which it brings to man she finds a real display of something unquestionably divine. Just as in her poetry she extends
the significance of actual things and events by seeing in them a
symbolical significance which reaches into vaster and less familiar

spheres, so in her religious beliefs she sees in the physical world not only something powerful and life-giving in itself but the symbol of something else still more powerful and more life-giving. She does not distinguish between the importance of things in themselves and their importance symbolically, because for her this importance is one and the same. The physical world is separated from the spiritual by artificial barriers, and for some the distinction may be meaningless. With her acute and lively senses Miss Sitwell sees in the events of physical nature the manifestations of a spiritual power, and this is the inspiration of her faith and the object of her worship.

An example of this outlook can be seen in Miss Sitwell's treatment of light. Light is an ancient symbol for the dazzling radiance of God and has many implications for the faithful. But the light of which they speak is usually the 'celestial light' which Milton summoned to irradiate his soul. For Miss Sitwell celestial and physical light are one; the sun is a power both in the physical world and in the spirit. It is—

The Sun whose body was spilt on our fields to bring us harvest, and it is also a divine power which resolves the discords of life and imparts an order to everything:

> to him, the heat of the earth
> And beat of the heart are one,—
> Born from the energy of the world, the love
> That keeps the Golden Ones in their place above,
> And hearts and blood of beasts even in motion.

Just as in spring the sun revives decayed life and creates hope in men and women, so in the spirit something similar happens when 'the Intelligible Light' works its miraculous transformations and turns all to gold. And this identification of the physical with the spiritual is true not only to the intellect but to the heart. The warmth which we receive from the sun in spring, and the sudden burst of hopes and affections which it brings, are not purely physical sensations. In our complex natures body and soul are so intermixed that they cannot ultimately be distinguished, and what affects the one affects the other. That is why in "Holiday" Miss

Sitwell shows how the whole natural and human scene is transformed by the power of light:

> Beneath the flowering boughs of heaven
> The country roads are made of thickest gold;
> They stretch beyond the world, and light like snow
> Falls where we go, the Intelligible Light
> Turns all to gold, the apple, the dust, the unripe wheat-ear.

And this visible transformation is only part of a greater transformation which affects the human consciousness no less than the countryside. The same power brings men closer to one another, makes men and women fall in love, sanctifies the commonest human feelings, and banishes despair and doubt. This miraculous change can only be called divine, and that is why Miss Sitwell, true to her convictions, associates it with symbols of Christian belief, and shows how—

> the workless hands
> Where the needs of famine have grown the claws of the lion
> Bear now on their palms the wounds of the Crucified,

or finds in so simple an act as the gift of a crumb to a starving bird a symbol of the breaking of the Body of Christ.

The depth of these convictions gives a peculiar strength to such a poem as "How Many Heavens." Starting from the words of John Donne that 'the Stancarest will needs have God not only to be in everything but to be everything,' Miss Sitwell pursues her own line of thought and tells how her blood responds to the growing grass, as if it were the display of a divine power. Then she tells how she finds God in the flame and the shadow, in the stone, the straw and the light, and comes to her exalted conclusion:

> He is the sea of ripeness, and the sweet apple's emerald's
> lore.
> So you, my flame of grass, my root of the world from which
> all Spring shall grow,
> O you, my hawthorn bough of the stars, now leaning now
> Through the day, for your flowers to kiss, my lips shall know

> *He is the core of the heart of love, and He, beyond labouring*
> *seas, our ultimate shore.*

The divine power, which is revealed in natural things and through
them restores the heart of man, is in the end love. That is why it
is a source of healing and of strength, why it sustains men against
their blackest misgivings and redeems them from their brutal faults.
It is this love for which the poet prays in "Invocation," though it
may seem for the moment to be almost beyond her call:

> *Now falls the night of the world: O Spirit moving upon the*
> *waters*
> *Your peace instil*
> *In the animal heat and splendour of the blood.*

It is this which in "Green Song" blesses all things 'in their poor
earthy dress' and makes men conscious of their forgotten faiths
and delights and duties. It is this which in "An Old Woman"
brings comfort to a woman in her old age and makes her see that
there is an easy answer to many questions which have troubled
her and a consolation for the losses which have been hers. It is
this which brings comfort to those who have lost their beauty,
their youth, their children, their wives, to the haunted and the
hunted, the misfits and the outcasts, the victims of social injus-
tice and of pitiless carnage. Whatever wounds mankind may
inflict upon itself, whatever it may suffer from decay and destitution, it can in the end be healed by finding itself in harmony
with the powers of nature and with the light and the love that
inform them.

This is Miss Sitwell's answer to the dark questions raised by
the war. Though in many of the poems she does not refer directly
to it and even seems to have dismissed it from her thoughts, it is
never really far from her. It raises the problems which she has to
solve and it provides the bitter experience of suffering which makes
her heart and mind so alert and so quick to understand the agonies
of others. Her own conflict has been between the heart and the
mind, between the blood and the bone. While her tender heart
has drawn her into the storm of human afflictions and tossed her

31

about in their chaos, her mind has wished to keep its distance and its detachment. In "Heart and Mind" she suggests that this conflict can never really be ended until the end of the world. Yet she herself has done much to resolve it. Her heart has forced her mind to take note of the sufferings of men and to widen its understanding until beyond the immediate horrors of the present it can see a not impossible future when human sympathies will revive and heal old wounds. It finds even in the destruction of life a means for its redemption. And she herself is perhaps conscious of such a solution. For in "Song," after telling how she has lost her old world and found an empty substitute for it, she concludes:

> For withering my heart, that summer rose,
> Came another heart like a sun,—
> And it drank all the dew from the rose, my love,
> And the birds have forgotten their song
> That sounded all summer long, my dear—
> All the bright summer long.

Her new heart, which has withered so much in her, and robbed her of her old songs, is none the less like a sun and gives its life and strength to her.

EDITH SITWELL

Frederic Prokosch

The prevalent taste and practice of poetry in England has, during the last six years or so (during the war, let us say) moved in a strikingly different direction from that in America: in America, a consolidation of the Auden influence (actually more congenial to America than England)—a body of didactic, crisp, experimental verse of various types, and a revulsion against the elegiac, the sensuous, the lyrical; in England on the other hand a powerful reaction against Auden, and a resurgence of traditional influences, of traditional imagery and metrics.

Two figures seem most largely associated with this tendency: Dylan Thomas and Edith Sitwell. Both are cryptic, incantatory poets (in their recent work) and both employ a highly developed system of symbols quite unlike Auden's, quite removed from everyday life, highly nostalgic and almost archaic; both are superlative craftsmen.

But Dylan Thomas uses extremely regular, tightly knit forms, both in idiom and metrics; Edith Sitwell's poems of the last several years (those in *Green Song* and *The Song of the Cold*) employ a flowing, opulent, declamatory manner and meter, which I should think would be particularly alien to contemporary American taste. Her position in England has risen tremendously, however.

Unquestionably her most recent poems are her best. In fact, they have risen from the level of badinage and ornamentation to

33

that of real grandiloquence, in the best sense. And her early poems, it seems to me, now take on a new value, for one can see in them now the roots of that elaborate imagery and meditative lyricism which has flowered so weirdly, so astonishingly in her latest work. The whole vocabulary has taken on a new depth and intensity, in fact a whole new level of significance. The recurring symbols (the Rose, the Ape, the Lion, the Worm) have grown into something very rich and very powerful.

What is really most impressive of all, as one compares the early poems with the late, is the remarkable growth in facility, the flawless ear, and the loose, long, undulating yet wonderfully precise phrasing; only years of zealous craftsmanship can produce this kind of clear, stately felicity:

> I, an old woman whose heart is like the sun
> That has seen too much, looked on too many sorrows,
> Yet is not weary of shining, fulfilment and harvest
> Heard the priests that howled for rain and the universal darkness,
> Saw the golden princess sacrificed to the Rain-god,
> The cloud that came, and was small as the hand of Man,

Or this:

> Though dust, the shining racer, overtake me,
> I too was a golden woman like those that walk
> In the fields of the heavens: but am now grown old
> And must sit by the fire and watch the fire grow cold . . .

And, of course, the thing that supports and justifies this splendor of phrase and posture is the depth of feeling that one feels in almost every line; it is intensely emotional poetry, and in this respect likewise completely alien to the present American tradition. Poems like "The Poet Laments the Coming of Old Age," "An Old Woman," "Eurydice," "A Mother to Her Dead Child," and "A Song of the Cold," are first of all the outpourings of passion, authoritative and unashamed, graced with the austerity of old age. These poems, certainly, fall into the main body of English poetry, and rise far above fashion and contemporaneity.

34

Miss Sitwell, like Yeats, stands as a shining and awe-inspiring example of how a poet, after a prolonged and sometimes hesitant apprenticeship, can finally in old age acquire his true idiom, can strike so to speak at the real core of his inspiration at last, and can produce, even in the tragic and despairing meditations of old age, a passionate, resonant, triumphant justification of a long career.

THE RECENT PROSE AND POETRY
OF EDITH SITWELL

Horace Gregory

Edith Sitwell's collection of poems, *The Song of the Cold*, London, 1945, is only just about to be published in this country. Even now it would seem that American critics who have weight with publishers as well as editorial advisors are still shy of Miss Sitwell's merits in the writing of poetry. In an age when imaginative writing is rare this particular shyness seems extraordinary; one looks for a reason to explain the phenomenon, and perhaps one reason of several is that Miss Sitwell's art has the appearance of seeming "unfashionable." It must be admitted that for the past fifteen years or so, Miss Sitwell's writings have been independent of critical "styles" and attitudes, and the curious phenomenon of criticism in the United States is that its highest "fashions" usually trail twenty years behind the moment of imaginative perception. This does no great harm to the poet, for the effort to be "in style" is far more harmful than the lack of immediate recognition, and here Miss Sitwell herself has a few words to say concerning the critical "fashions" of our time, "when inspiration is regarded with suspicion, and form is derided as old-fashioned, as if there could be fashion in poetry: such an idea degrades the art to the level of a dressmaker's shop—" and so it does.

At the present moment Miss Sitwell's gifts seem to be "less lonely" than they were ten years ago. In certain quarters and on both sides of the Atlantic something very like a neo-romantic

36

temper is finding speech. At Miss Sitwell's right hand one discerns the figures of Walter de la Mare and the late W. B. Yeats, and at her left, the Anglo-Welsh poet, Dylan Thomas, whose *Deaths and Entrances* is among the best of recent books of poems published in England. In saying this I do not mean that Miss Sitwell has joined a literary "movement,"—but for those who enjoy making terms (which never, of course, define the individual character of a poet's imagination) the word, "neo-romantic," is less confusing than others.

So much then for the more general and temporal atmosphere that Miss Sitwell's prose and poetry inhabit. But more important than their emergence among books of like temperament are their affinities to Baroque art, which Roger Fry has so happily defined as "the utmost possible enlargement of a unit of design—" and in saying this Roger Fry was speaking of El Greco. I have written elsewhere[1] of the relationship of Miss Sitwell's poetry to "the Baroque idea" and of its affinity to the poetry of Richard Crashaw; and those elements which define the Baroque imagination are also witnessed in her prose. Those who wish to understand whatever may seem "obscure" in Miss Sitwell's poems should turn to similar situations and "keepings" in her three books of prose: *Alexander Pope* (1930), *Victoria of England* (1936), and *Fanfare for Elizabeth* (1946). In her *Alexander Pope* she selected five lines from his "Ode on Saint Cecilia's Day" and she remarked upon their "splendor:"

> *Thy stone, O Sisyphus, stands still,*
> *Ixion rests upon his wheel*
> *And the pale spectres dance;*
> *The Furies sink upon their iron beds,*
> *And snakes uncurl'd hang list'ning round their heads.*

In "Girl and Butterfly" (one of Miss Sitwell's recent poems) the echo and reflection of Pope's lines are heard and seen:

> *I, an old man,*
> *Bent like Ixion on my broken wheel the world,*

[1]The "Vita Nuova" of Baroque Art in the Recent Poetry of Edith Sitwell. Poetry, Vol. LXVI. June 1945.

37

> Stare at the dust and scan
> What has been made of it ...

And in still another of her recent poems, the image of Pope's Sisyphus is reilluminated:

> An old man weary with rolling wisdom like a stone
> Up endless hills to lay on the innocent eyes
> Said, 'Once I was Plato, wise
> In the ripe and unripe weathers of the mind,

*   *   *

The same relationship exists between a passage in *Fanfare for Elizabeth* and several of her recent poems. It is characteristic of Miss Sitwell's method in her *Elizabeth* to quote Thomas Dekker's commentary (remembered from his childhood) on Elizabethan London:

> At length a blinde Bear was tyed to the stake, and instead of baiting him with dogges, a company of creatures that had the shapes of men, and faces of Christians, (being either Colliers, Carters, or Watermen) took the office of Beadles upon them, and whipt Mounsier Hunkes, till the blood ran doune his old shoulders it was some sport to see Innocence triumph over Tyranny, by beholding those unnecessary tormentors go away with scratched hands or torne legs from a porre Beast arm'd only by nature to defend himself against Violence ...

If we turn to *The Song of the Cold* and open its pages to her justly admired poem, "Still Falls the Rain," the parallel "keepings" are to be found:

> In the self-murdered heart, the wounds of the sad uncom-
>   prehending dark,
> The wounds of the baited bear,—
> The blind and weeping bear whom the keepers beat
> On his helpless flesh ...

And in "O bitter love, O Death ..." there are the following lines,

38

'*I was a great gold-sinewed King, I had a lion's mane*
Like the raging Sun . . .

These have their parallel in *Fanfare for Elizabeth* through
Miss Sitwell's Henry VIII, his "leonine strength" . . . and . . .
"Even in his later years Henry had still an appearance of great
magnificence and power, like a sun running to seed."

Parallels such as these could be quoted in great number from
passages of Miss Sitwell's poetry and prose, which is another way
of saying that all her later writings are singularly unified, that
they are interwoven in such fashion as to provide their own commentary upon the text, all without apology or lengthy annotation.

Perhaps it would be pertinent to say that Miss Sitwell's books
in prose, her *Pope*, her *Victoria*, her *Bath*, London (1932), her
Fanfare for Elizabeth, are neither histories nor biographies. They
are dramatic essays upon chosen subjects that have attracted her
critical perception. Not unlike an insight that is peculiarly her
own—yet by virtue of her poetry (for Saint-Beuve's talents for
writing verse were frail and undistinguished) she sustains a notable
advantage over her famous predecessor.

It is "the Baroque idea" that Miss Sitwell has mastered and
in prose her "unit of design" has been of the same proportions that
are to be found in a number of her poems. Each of her canvases
is of moderate size: her *Victoria* has the innocent appearance of
being a domestic study of the Queen; her *Elizabeth* holds at its
center the relationship between Anne Boleyn and Henry VIII—
but in both essays it is the "utmost enlargement of a unit of design"
within the canvas that gives the portrait meaning. In *Victoria of
England* the Queen and her Prince Consort, Albert, are in the
foreground, but the significant backdrops to the scene are Karl
Marx's Birmingham, Manchester and London, and which, of
course, are equally "Victorian." If the Prince Consort was aware
of the scenes behind him (for among the causes of his early death
was overwork in fulfilling his offices of philanthropy) the Queen
was not: much of what she saw was seen in the far and romantic
perspectives visible from a Palace window or from the lawns of
Balmoral in Scotland. She beheld the rise and fall of her ministers with the equanimity of one who saw beyond them into the far

reaches of the British Empire, and because Disraeli had divined that look into far distances, its meanings and its vanities, he made his Victoria Empress of India.

From *Victoria of England* to *Fanfare for Elizabeth* the distance is not so great as it may seem: both Queens are symbols of victorious wars, and of comparative success in maintaining monarchical prestige and power,—all these associations are obvious, and need not be elaborated. But a subtler connection between the two Queens exists and it is one that is characteristic of Miss Sitwell's perceptions as well as her approach to matters of historical scholarship. The nature of her scholarship is not of a sort that reassures the literal-minded, placates those who know all the answers before questions arise, and finally sends a patient reader off to sleep. Her sources have never been the usual source of historical supplies—those huge, and often gray warehouses where historical platitudes are stored and treasured. In *Fanfare for Elizabeth*, Miss Sitwell acknowledges her debt to the half-gotten genius of two of Queen Victoria's favorite subjects, Agnes and Eliza Strickland. Granted that the Misses Strickland were predisposed in favor of royal prerogatives, that they were champions of the lost cause of the Stuarts, their two great works, *Lives of the Queens of Scotland* and *Lives of the Queens of England*, contain a larger body of documented fact than is to be found in the more eloquent, more stridently political (since his interpretations seldom varied from a Whig "party line") histories of Lord Macaulay. Through patronage of the Queen's ministers, the Strickland sisters secured access to court documents on both sides of the English channel; they were discursive and industrious in selecting "evidence" and they were not adverse to quoting rare fragments of court poetry to substantiate their arguments; they had a passion for giving their readers the minutiae of domestic life; as though they were female twin Balzacs, they uncovered through the medium of rare letters, small, casually recorded actions, and details of dress and manner, the hidden motives of feminine and worldly behavior.

In this century it has remained for Miss Sitwell to rediscover the true merits of the Strickland biographies, to find what is excellent within them, and to set aside Strickland discursiveness in favor

of the psychological detail which the historian's seemingly tireless
devotion to her task had brought to the surface of a crowded page.[2]

With the Misses Strickland as her Victorian authorities Miss
Sitwell's Elizabethan essay is on the forces that made Elizabeth
what she was to become—a "Virgin Queen," mindful from adoles-
cence onward of a heritage of bloodshed, of loose-tongued scan-
dal, of the aging sun-King Henry, of the confused emotions
wakened by the attentions paid to her by Admiral Lord Seymour
when she was far too young to receive them with propriety. The
book in itself is no longer than an uncut version of an Elizabethan
play—and its presentation is no less concentrated and dramatic.
Of the violence that preceded Elizabeth's arrival on the throne,
Miss Sitwell quotes the Queen's own words that were spoken
many years later, two years before her death, "Mortua sed non
sepulta. Mortua sed non sepulta."

A question might well be asked concerning the relevance of
Miss Sitwell's gifts to twentieth century poetry. In a final sense
much of her recent poetry has a "timeless" air, and in the best
sense of the term it is "traditional," which is to say that it renews
an aspect of English poetry which came to light in the sixteenth
and seventeenth centuries, that had been revived by Chatterton
and Keats, by Thomas Lovell Beddoes, that illuminated the best
lines of Tennyson as well as the best of Hopkins and of Swinburne
—all variously gifted poets and unlike one another—yet each con-
tributed to what is loosely known as "romanticism," the Diony-
sian aspect of English poetry. It is that line with its heritage of
myth and legend, its images of love among the ruins, of life-in-
death, the conceit of the rose springing from the grave which
enters Edith Sitwell's poetry. One might say that the theme of
life-in-death which haunts passages of Coleridge's "Ancient

_____

[2] In Una Pope-Henessey's biography of Agnes and Eliza Strickland, there is
a camera portrait of Agnes Strickland in 1864, heavily bonneted and shawled,
as she appeared before under-graduates at Oxford, who greeted her with
cheers of "The Queens! The Queens! The Queens!" Not unlike those critics
who underrated Trollope as a mere business man among novelists, adverse
critics of Agnes and Eliza Strickland saw them as business women of historical research and therefore underrated the wealth of "evidence" which sup-
ported their deeply penetrating character studies of the Queens of England.

Mariner" is one of the principal themes that is variously presented and renewed in Miss Sitwell's *The Song of the Cold*, and which gives that volume its character of "timelessness," of a being apart from merely immediate associations of so much so-called "modern poetry." Its individual distinctions, its limitations and disciplines are those of the "Baroque idea," and within that definition no poet of the twentieth century can be brought into comparison with Edith Sitwell. But the question still remains as to how her poetry discloses one of the hidden and rooted sensibilities of our day, and why her recent poetry and prose cannot be described as an "escape" from the present, but holds a mirror up to a scene that reflects the temper of the mid-twentieth century. In Europe the two great wars have reawakened the presence of death, and among scenes of destruction, Europe's "romantic" past has been unearthed and has been revived in human consciousness as well as in its physical reality. The blacked-out countrysides and cities restored the presence of an almost medieval night, and a physical darkness in which half-forgotten myths and legends renewed their hold upon the imagination. As in all periods when wars and revolutions are in the air, the radical centers of both daily life and imaginative being are brought into view, and in that upheaval, the view is scarcely one of classical restraint, but rather one in which the very roots of being, the roots of human good and evil, are exposed. It is this respect that certain aspects of the past enter the present and are at one with it, and it is characteristic of Miss Sitwell's sensibility to reilluminate a passage from one of John Donne's sermons, "that God is an angel in an angel, and a stone in a stone, and a straw in a straw," in her poem "How Many Heavens . . ."

One need not labor the point (and it would be gratuitous to do so) that "How Many Heavens . . ." is a devotional poem of unusual excellence, or that its art embraces "the Baroque idea," or that its music and its imagery revive those qualities which we associate with the late renaissance in English poetry. For us the atmosphere which Miss Sitwell's recent poetry creates may well be called "neo-romantic" because it presents a contrast to "neo-classical fashions" in contemporary criticism. Since Miss Sitwell

42

herself has disclaimed the relevance of all critical "fashions" to poetry, it is not extraordinary that her poetry exists without reference to them. And it would seem that by ignoring the critical "fashions" of her day she offers a salutary example to a younger generation of British and American poets.

THE LATEST POEMS OF EDITH SITWELL

Jack Lindsay

Edith Sitwell's poetry since 1945 has taken a sharp turn. There is indeed a close relation in many ways between these post-war poems and those written during the war; and if one presses the point, one can find elements reaching far back into her early work. But that is only to say that Edith Sitwell is a poet and her work makes up a living whole from start to finish. Within that whole these postwar poems hold a definite place all their own.

At a glance they have breadth, a prophetic certainty of statement, to which one is tempted to give a term often used in a vague way to cover vaguely aspiring writing: cosmic. For they deal in manifest immensities:

> *Upon great yellow flags and banners of the ancient Cold*
> *Began the huge migrations . . .*

so opens "The Shadow of Cain." "Street Acrobat" opens:

> *Upon the shore of noon, the wide azoic*
> *Shore of diamonds where no wave comes, sprawled the*
> *   nation*

And this largeness appears even in the metre, in which predominates a long line of tumbling oceanic cadences. The imagery tends to be sharply elemental, even at times drawn from the more remote abstractions of philosophy.

44

> *But the cold is the highest mathematical idea . . . the Cold*
> *is Zero—*
> *The Nothing from which arose*
> *By all Being and all variation. . . .*

These first impressions are confirmed by careful re-reading; but they are seen to embrace only certain aspects of the poems. There is no sentimental or yearning loss of the contours of thought and feeling in dimensions beyond or below human experience. Those dimensions are continually evoked, but as the background, the foreground, the inground (to invent a term as a sort of variation of Hopkins' *inscape*) of the deepest conflicts of our world.

These poems both complete certain imagic and rhythmic trends present in Edith Sitwell's work from the outset and lift her whole definition on to a new level. To bring out their significance one needs to understand something of the full movement of her work from 1916 on and to realise the cultural situation in England out of which it arose and on which it impacted. That is a long story; but for the purposes of this essay a few brief generalisations can be made. On the one hand Edith Sitwell in her early work was expressing a general phase of dissident European *avant-garde* culture (which involved *symbolisme*, Apollinaire, cubism, fauvism, and the multiple potentialities gathered under the name of futurism; and which was given a particular concentration of revolt by the 1914-8 war). But on the other hand she was concerned with the English situation, English culture; and that meant a need to break through the impasse reached by the Georgian poets, who had thought to reinvigorate English poetry and reach the "common man" by such expedients as the colloquialising of Victorian forms. They could not see that the "common man" they thus sought to reach was the child of Victorian philistinism and represented the death of poetry.

Edith Sitwell's early work blasted through the Georgian impasse. To the Georgians and the critics she seemed a mere furious destroyer drawing on foreign sources for method; but in fact she was at every point closely related to the vital tradition of English poetry and was seeking for uncontaminated community.

45

It was precisely because her poetry had such deep and thriving roots in the English past and present that her impact was so decisive, so destructive, so revitalising. Those she destroyed may be forgiven for having seen only the destructive aspects; but a generation later than the advent of *wheels* we can now evalue the nutritive forces in her work, which has created a totally new poetic climate in England.

Wheels and the Dada of Geneva were contemporaries; and one important aspect of Edith Sitwell's work is that with her, explosively, along an extending line of activity, English poetry rejoins the Europeans stream of development and rediscovers the meaning of revolt and community. France during the 19th and 20th centuries has been many eddies, leaps, gaps, in poetic movement; but from Baudelaire and De Nerval up to the present moment there has been a steady reaffirmation of the creative role of the poet amid the changing historical pressures. After Keats, Shelley and Byron, that tradition died out in England. Edith Sitwell therefore could not appeal to even the narrow remnants of a dissident creative movement; she could look back to Blake, Keats, Coleridge, but between her and them yawned the Victorian death.

Along some such lines we may measure the tremendous difficulties of the task she confronted and the depth of creative powers which enabled her to triumph in such a situation.

II

She had to pick up the last strands of the true Romantic tradition in England, and then redefine that tradition in terms of the world about her and herself in that world. In harmony with this need was her response to the European *avantgarde* elements already mentioned. She was able to bring the focus of Rimbaud and Appollinaire to bear on her task without loss of personal or national orientation.

Breaking through the phoney harmonies of the Georgians she revealed the truth of sensibility in her world, the hell under the pretences, the jangling discords under the lie of reconcilia-

46

tion. The world dissolved into a jagged fury of conflicting planes, with the senses confounded in the vortex of the hidden trauma. Confronted with the lie and the pang, the simian world fell into its rich patterns of decomposition; or stood x-rayed in brittle grinding oppositions.

But because this vision of hell was poetically realised, it bore at its own heart the potences of heaven. The poetic act is the marriage of heaven and hell, as Blake knew. The harsh edges turned into the delimiting factors of a new harmony true to the human condition. The trauma, exposed to the Apollinian light, provided the basis for a new health. The dissociation, dominant in the world, was overcome and made to yield the secret of a new integration. An integration, not a phoney bit of wishful-thinking based on the veiling of the deep conflict, but proceeding out of the heart of that conflict.

Both heaven and hell receded into the small and complete garden of childhood; and the gigantic struggle of alienating and integrating forces in the world was telescoped into the formative process of the senses in the magicked child. The return to the pure sources expressed the healing of the trauma, and now out of a delicate unfolding of dream-movement the poet dared to move through the complex maze of associations into the realising structure of symbol.

In symbol the poet gets to the root of the uniting factor in man. And so from this point Edith Sitwell moved back into the world of actual men and women, able to hold fast to her gains (the free poetic image truly based in the human condition) and yet able to express sympathy. To feel and express sympathy for men and women in the rending and yet partly-resolved struggle of everyday life. Community has been found anew. Not the tainted good-fellowship of the Georgians, which hoped to conjure away the evil of the world with a clap on the back and a hearty drink in the village-pub. But the fullness of poetic union.

The wheel has come round full circle. But what is achieved is not a return, but a new start.

III

Two points in this progress are of special importance for the present inquiry. "Gold Coast Customs," and the war poems.

"Gold Coast Customs" stands for the moment when the stark realisation of hell (*Facade*) mates with the lovely dream of lost Edens (*The Sleeping Beauty*), and out of the marriage of heaven and hell the Earth of Man is simply, terribly, exaltingly begotten.

In this movement a new enrichment of the time-planes occurs. Two moments of horror—one primitive, one contemporary—are fused, but not in mechanical superimposition. The effect is of violent contrary movements, a nausea-sudden fall back through levels of time into a ghastly and hopeless centre of fear and a forward-movement out of the engulfing past into the crisis-moment of renewal. Cain, Dives, and Christ (basic symbols for Edith Sitwell of the human condition and the forms of social struggle that make up history) now appear. Cain or Dives seems victorious; the seamless garment of man is rent and divided up among the hirelings; and yet the Whole Man lives on and reasserts himself, in the toil that makes bread and the pang that makes poetry. "The fires of God go marching on."

In the war-poems the same complex of attitudes is revived and extended. Pity deepens, and the time-planes become more complex. The image of elemental death and renewal grows surer, and is made one with the deepest elements in human experience. The battle of men is realised, not as somthing projected on to the detached screen of the universe, but as a storm of potences which reaches everywhere. A form of pantheism? Yes, but not quite according to the definitions in the manuals of philosophy. Pantheisms have usually been of a passive contemplative nature; and this attitude is essentially active. Man and nature are felt as one only because man is discovered at the deep polarising levels of his basic conflicts and integrations, of the process that makes him man. The philosophic affinity is rather with Marx who says that, in the development whereby man's natural existence becomes his human existence, "nature has become man for him."

48

When our war in "Out Danced the Babioun" is expressed as a pterodactyl fouling its own nest, we feel more than an allergy of regression. We feel a poetry in which air-raid and monstrous prehistoric combat have been imaginatively brought together by a valid system of symbolically realised correspondences.

IV

In "The Shadow of Cain" and related poems written since 1945 Edith Sitwell brings together all the forces which I have outlined above in an effort to define the world of nuclear fission.

Nuclear fission is not for her a scientific discovery that just happened to be made, or that came out of a particular set of more or less accidental circumstances. In the key of the attitude I have discussed as her resting-point (a kind of humanist-pantheism) she inevitably sees it as both a physical and a human fact. It emerges from the total human process; and is one aspect of man's maturing grasp on the forces of himself and nature. She stands quite apart from the one-sided moralists who lament that man's ethical development lags behind his scientific, and sees that the scientific discovery is the very core of the moral problem. Here, in the discovery which lifts one great veil over the process of transformation, man confonts himself, his own good and evil. He confronts the terrific choice which is himself . From the political and economic angle this means a choice between using the physical powers for good or for evil, for productive or for destructive purposes; but poetically it means a penetration to those deep polarising levels at which the conflict between fear and desire, death and life, dissociation and unity, forever go on.

This is the rending moment of choice and conflict which she sets out in "The Shadow" and the other poems. From one angle the poems define the deep timeless processes of growth; from another angle they define the agonisingly immediate issues of the use of atomic power. Because of the tensions between these two aspects—the timeless and the socially-engaged—these poems gain their great force, and are so extremely important to our culture.

49

Briefly, "The Shadow" restates in the new historical situation the conflict posed by "Gold Coast Customs." But because of the new breadths of realisation, the necessary involvement of physics as well as history, the contrasted-and-united planes are not only those of primitive and of contempory life. There is vast geologic recession of planes, which gives the element of cosmic bleakness that I referred to at the outset. And this massing of huge simple convolutions and retreating diagonals of force is one with certain dream-structures of space. The crucial evolutionary moment, the moment of fundamental scientific discovery of the nature of energy-matter-process, the moment of human change and renewal (in both individual and group)—all these moments are fused together in the imagery and rhythm of the poem.

Since this poem has been found difficult of comprehension, perhaps I may be permitted to give an outline of its themes.

It opens with a broad statement (in Hegelian terms) of the issue from the focus of physics, which is linked with the picture of geologic phases of convulsive movement—we are at the molecular level as well as in a dream-space. Man emerges (as in a primitive myth such as that of the Zuni). Man in his primitive ritual finds his precarious unity with the vast forces; and through the imagery of the birth-trauma relates his own experience to his intuitions of elemental change. Beyong terror he arrives at regeneration; the panic power breaks into the realisation of human renewal and the rejection of division:

> And the great rolling world-wide thunders of that drumming
>   underground
> Proclaim our Christ, and roar: 'Let there be harvest!
> Let there be no more Poor—
> For the Son of God is sowed in every furrow!'

And so we are suddenly in our own world, where the deepest processes of spiritual transformation, symbolised as Christ, have suddenly appeared as the knowledge of nuclear fission, a new deepening of the knowledge of good and evil. But the evil has got out of hand:

> The Primal Matter
> Was broken, the womb from which all life began,
> Then to the murdered Sun a totem pole of dust arose in
> memory of Man.

The forces of terror have gained control; and we go falling, falling,
aeon after aeon . . .
> Life is split to the core. And there:

> in that hollow lay the body of our brother
> Lazarus, upheaved from the world's tomb.

The poor man, the maker of bread who is also the living wheat-
car, the murdered man around whom the forces of redemption
most powerfully play. To him hurry "the civilisation of the
Maimed, and, too, Life's Lepers." They cry for salvation, in the
midst of terrible pressures of regression. "Then Dives was brought
. . . He lay like a leprous Sun."

> Like a great ear of wheat that is swoln with grain
> Then ruined by white rain.

There lie the two dead men, who are Man, with their conflicting
forces, their opposed symbols of *gold* (Gold that is quick of light
in the corn, alchemic moment of transmutation and the healing
of all sores, money the faecal defilement and the fires of corruption). And the golds fight and unite; the opposed forces are
broken down into a new unity; the fission in man, reaching down
through all levels, is made the basis of a new wholeness. Because
the horror is faced and understood at all levels, Christ arises out
of the split sepulchre and womb. A Judgment Day of all that
distorted and divided; an achievement of peace, plenty, brother-
hood.

V

The other poems explore related aspects of this theme. "The
Coat of Fire," for instance, concentrates on the terrific pressures
of good and evil, regression and integration, in the moment of
choice which is the sole human reality at this moment.

> Some doomed to descend
> Through all the hells and change into the Dog
> Without its faithfulness, the Crocodile
> Without its watchfulness, and then to Pampean mud.
> In the circles of the city's hells beneath the fog
> These bear, to light them, in the human breast
> The yellow dull light from the raging human dust,
> The dull blue light from the brutes, light red as rust
> Of blood from eyeless weeping ghosts, light black as smoke,
> From hell. . . .

This poem, in which a heavy hand seems to weigh remorselessly down on the mind and body as one reads, breaks too on its cry of pity and its red noon of Judgment Day. Street Acrobat concentrates on the dangerous swaying moment over the abysses of time, the anguish of the realisation in which alone lies safety, and the buoyant blind rush of life that is blithely unaware of the awful struggle on which all depends. "Chain-Gang: Penal Settlement" opens "Go down, red Sun, red Cain!" and reverberates to a heavy beat of pain and toil; and prophesies a reversal of things, a redemption into unity. "Dirge for the New Sunrise" is a direct cry against the absolute murder of Man by the use of the atomic bomb, a use linked with all the greeds, fears, hates which have allowed men to batten on their fellows:

> Bound to my heart as Ixion to the wheel,
> Nailed to my heart as the Thief upon the Cross
> I hang between our Christ and the gap where the world
>   was lost
> And watch the phantom Sun in Famine Street . . .

VI

These poems, sibylline in their strange intensity of sustained revelation, are then both a sudden new development in Edith Sitwell's art and the natural consequence of her earliest work. In her movement between 1916 and 1948 we witness the kind of growth possibly only in a great poet. That movement in one

52

sense belongs to a general European development, within which it has certain affinities with the forces of revolt and integration to be seen in the work of Tzara and Eluard. But it is also English in its essential bearings; and has operated by a deepening of personal sensibility which at the same time finds points of contact with the most vital elements in our vast poetry—in the great Romantics, the Metaphysicals (whom we would do better to call Symbolists) of the 17th century, the medieval visionaries from Langland to Dunbar, the elements of dance and fantasy in the popular tradition which includes Skelton and Nursery Rhymes, Folkplay and broadsheet ballad. She has thus succeeded in building a bridge back over the heads of the Victorians to the living past, as well as opening doors to the future.

In these latest poems she has carried the concentration and refinement of her poetic powers beyond a point where one can talk of influences. In one sense she is aware of Blake and Donne (of the Sermons and *Devotions*); but that is only an expression of her sure roots in our tradition. Donne's sense of symbolic correspondences between man and the universe, and Blake's capacity to create a structure of myth fusing personal experience, organic imagery, historical event, scientific thesis, do indeed reappear here in new guises, but that is because Edith Sitwell triumphantly completes her demolition of the false, her contact with the living past, and her movement into the integration without which men are doomed.

53

THE GARDEN AND THE HARVEST

John Piper

If Edith Sitwell asked me to design her a monument I should include somewhere in an elaborate abstract composition a number of symbolic objects: a rose, half real and half jewelled, a garden gate with a spider's web filling in the arch above it, a burning glass and a "corn-maiden", a pagan harvest fertility symbol still to be found in the porches of some rural English churches.

Once, as a girl—perhaps a very little girl—inside a garden, Edith Sitwell's senses must have had some sudden blow, enduring in its effect. Probably the blow has hammered at her senses many times since; probably it still hammers. But her poetry gives me the impression that she has at some time experienced one all-revealing moment which, as she goes on writing, she gets nearer and nearer to recapturing. In her most recent work she has come very near to re-living the all-revealing moment. The moment was one of intense apprehension of ripening life, giving a realisation not only of Lear's "ripeness is all" but also of the exact nature of personal and universal ripeness. Concerned with the moment, she sees sunshot walls of brick and rich-textured stone, scarlet flowers, golden fruit, perhaps hears a voice drifting from the lake through the warm yellow air, or a movement or a sound of music: the moment has become for her the measure of all poetry and all passion for ever.

In the early poems a fairy-tale life goes on: elegant, witty and fragile. Fragments of legend and myth contribute to it. An eclec-

54

tic magic is woven into the poems. Comments on outside life are oblique, naivety and sophistication wear each other's disguises self-consciously as they face life on the other side of the wall—that other side that can only be approached by breaking the spider's web and scattering the dewdrops. The senses—the voice, the fingers, the eyes—all enjoy an elaborate richness of design and effect. Is the poet heartless, like the Snow Queen? Her Winter is brittle and unreal; her Spring, though rainwashed and tender, is remote as a Japanese print or a song from *A Winter's Tale*; but the full ripe words concerned with late Summer and Autumn beat, even in that jewelled world, with the reality and the passion that is to be developed in the poems written since 1939. For always

> the heat of the earth
> And beat of the heart are one.

And in that garden, jewelled with the cobwebs of Perrault, the power of evil belongs to the wicked Fairy, a fairy who, whether she is rushing backwards in time to the magic rituals of "The Golden Bough" to enlighten herself about the primitive fear of the unknown, or whether she is lingering on the way to becoming Circe or Cerberus or Pluto, is always horrid and always incalculable, but always outwitted by good. And iresistibly all the pleasure and pain from these sensuous moments, all the emotions of those strange half-pictorial half-literary conversation pieces are drawn like the rays of the sun through the burning glass of that early autumnal apprehension of life. And what a fire is started! To the burning glass the wall is no barrier. The rays beat down inside, outside, everywhere. For the garden is not after all a prison nor an escape from an ivory tower, but simply a place to be alone, a way of concentration.

Evil in the late poems is cold: nothing that is cold and sun-less can be drawn into the burning glass and kindle the fire. Cold is a grander, more terrifying thing than anything the capricious wicked fairy imagined; more potent, more stultifying. But cold can be overcome by fire and evil annihilated by the seasons in their cycle, and by the rich golden range of the harvest.

ON THE DEVELOPMENT OF
MISS SITWELL'S LATER STYLE

Kenneth Clark

Not even the most enthusiastic admirers of Miss Sitwell's earlier poetry—and the present writer has loved it since his school days—can have foreseen the development of her work during the last six or seven years. With the appearance of *Street Songs* and *Green Song*, those who care for poetry recognized a true poetic and prophetic cry which had not been heard in English since the death of Yeats. This was not merely exquisite poetry: it was great poetry; we felt once more the excitement of having amongst us a poet who could give us back our sight and our belief in the human heart, a poet on Shelley's definition. And, naturally, we are anxious to know by what steps this new eminence has been achieved.

Miss Sitwell's earlier poetry was written from a strange secluded world. We picture her imprisoned in an enormous kitchen garden where, to her childish eyes, the flowers, leaves and fruits are all of giant size. At one end of the garden is a summer house in the Chinese taste, faded and ramshackle, a few bells still tinkling from its eaves, and on its wallpaper, faintly discernible, Chinese ladies and gentlemen saluting one another with elegant *desinvoltura*. No human beings enter this garden, except a governess and an ancient, wrinkled gardener, who remains for long the most important figure in her imagination, but in the corner is a gazebo from which it is possible to catch sight of the neighbours, queer, country eccentrics, as they go to call on the great house.

In this garden the young lady lives in a kind of trance of sensuous receptivity. She sees, smells, touches and reads; and all her senses become confused and united. 'My senses', she wrote later, 'are like those of primitive peoples, at once acute and un-covered—and they are interchangeable!' This interchange is the ✓ basis of her early poetry. It accounts for the immediacy of her images, and from it develops that rarest of all sensibilities, the feeling for texture. When, long afterwards, Miss Sitwell writes of Pope that 'had his verses been transformed into flowers, he could have told lily from rose, buttercup from cowslip, in no matter how starless and moonless a night, merely from touching one petal', we can be sure that this is not critical fantasy, but a description of her own experience.

Picturing this young lady, we are reminded of another lonely child, nervous and over-bred, sitting in a forsaken garden, mesmer-ized by the sensuous quality of words, Algeron Charles Swinburne. Throughout Miss Sitwell's poetry a Swinburnian element persists. We are conscious of it in her elaborate technique, in her uncanny sensibility to the texture of language; and also, I dare say, in an occasional diffuseness, and in a feeling that the central core of her meaning is veiled in mist, and will dissolve if we approach it too closely. Miss Sitwell herself has accepted this kinship with Swinburne, and in the introduction to her anthology of Victorian poetry, she has described how the young lady from the enormous kitchen garden, complete with reluctant governess, laid a pagan offering, milk, honey and bay leaves, on the poet's tomb in the Isle of Wight. Miss Sitwell's appreciation of Swinburne's verbal mastery, which follows the account of her pilgrimage, is one of the most illuminating of all her critical studies, and one of the most personal. Many young people adored Swinburne in the early years of this century, but few mature poets would have ad-mitted to an equal admiration in 1932.

But this parallel must not be carried any further; for the essential limitation of Swinburne is that his mind never expanded; his emotions never deepened, and his genuinely poetic impulses were always those which had been absorbed in childhood and youth. He never grew up. The extraordinary fact about Miss

57

Sitwell, and the one which concerns us now, is that she did. We have no right to ask how Miss Sitwell came to leave her *hortus conclusus*. Perhaps she herself has given all the answer we need in a short poem called "Poor Young Simpleton":

> *Once my love seemed the Burning Bush*
> *The Pentecost Rushing of Flames;*
> *Now the Speech has fallen to the chatter of alleys*
> *Where fallen man and the rising ape*
> *And the howling Dark play games.*
> *For she leaned from the light like the Queen of Fairies*
> *Out of the bush of the yellow broom . . .*
> *'I'll take out that heart of yours,' she said,*
> *'And put in your breast a stone.*
> *'O, I'll leave an empty room,' she said,*
> *'A fouled, but an empty room.'*

The immediate results of this experience are expressed in that terrifying poem called "Gold Coast Customs," of which Miss Sitwell says, 'it was written with anguish, and I would not willingly relive that birth'. It is, in fact, a cry of horror at the spectacle of evil, and all the images of fear which have ever oppressed a nightmare, all the unspoken moments of horror which dustbins and back streets, old books of travel and ethnographical museums have stamped on the sensitive retina, are accumulated and repeated, as if there never could be enough to relieve the mind of its loathsome burden. The horror of the images is intensified by the terrifying tom-tom rhythms in which the poem is written, rhythms varying from the sinister rhythms of the jungle to the infinitely degraded, hollow, tom-tom rhythms of Jazz, the music of nothingness and futility. In spite of her anguish of spirit. Miss Sitwell has been able to command all the technical skill of what I may call her Chinoiserie poems; indeed, there was in these poems a peculiar spikiness of rhythm, and an occasional black shadow of sound which by a slight twist, were perfect instruments for her new purpose. As a work of art, "Gold Coast Customs" suffers from being too close to an appalling spiritual shock. It leaves us in the chaos of despair, and art is the opposite of chaos.

> But yet if only one soul would whine,
> Rat-like from the lowest mud, I should know
> That somewhere in God's vast love it would shine;
> But even the rat-whine has guttered low.

At the end there is a chink of hope, but it is vague, improbable and unsatisfying:

> Though Death has taken
> And pig-like shaken
> Rooted and tossed
> The rags of me.
> Yet the time will come
> To the heart's dark slum
> When the rich man's gold and the rich man's wheat
> Will grow in the street, that the starved may eat.

After "Gold Coast Customs," it is not surprising to find that Miss Sitwell wrote no poetry for many years. She was recreating her spirit, seeking a belief or a vision which would enable her to transcend the evil and misery in the world; and, during these years, evil was moving towards its catastrophe. We must suppose that much of her time was passed in reading, for these are the years of her anthologies of poetry with their critical introductions. And here I may say in parentheses that these introductions seem to me, within their self-imposed limits, to be among the most valuable pieces of modern criticism, and a merciful relief from that sheep in wolf's clothing, Taine's English Literature in a new disguise, the sociological criticism of Marxism. It is true that they endow the reader with a very subtle ear and demand from him very strict attention; and few readers, perhaps, can have followed Miss Sitwell in her discrimination of every nuance of sound. But anyone who has attempted to do so must have had his capacity for enjoying poetry increased beyond measure; and what more can we ask of criticism? As well as English poetry, her reading must have included Donne's sermons, Burton's Anatomy, St.

Thomas Aquinas, the Meister Eckhart and Schopenhauer; also the Homeric hymns, Pindar and other sources of classic ritual. It is as if, after the chaotic black magic, the tom-tom magic of "Gold Coast Customs, "she needed the white magic of the mystics or the golden magic of Demeter.

During this long night of poetic inspiration, or perhaps we should say this dread of accepting poetic inspiration, like a child who dare not sleep for fear of its dreams, Miss Sitwell also wrote a novel *I Live under a Black Sun*. In choosing for her subject the life of Jonathan Swift, the great protagonist of universal disgust, she was certainly guided by a therapeutic instinct, and some of her own horror and indignation were eased by absorption in the tragedy of this heroic nihilist. In the same spirit, she wrote descriptions of human wretchedness, more poignant than anything in "Gold Coast Customs," which show how closely the shock of her spirit had been connected with the spectacle of poverty. The novel also contains, to the bewilderment, it may well be of the regular novel reader, strange rhapsodic interludes, which seem like incidental music between the various sections of the narrative; and in these we feel that she is making her way back to poetry. Words and images float in and out, which are to reappear in "Street Songs"—the Potter's Field, the River of Lethe, the Man in Armour on the Roman Road, the Priests crying for Rain—and beyond these there are whole passages which are later to be reworked in poems.

I Live under a Black Sun was published in 1936. In the same year Miss Sitwell published a volume of collected poems in which the observant reader might have noticed one new poem, strangely different in style and content from the rest of the collection, significantly entitled "Prelude". In spite of very great beauties, it is not a completely successful poem: it is too literary, the fruit of too much reading. Many of its lines seem to come from an unknown classic of English literature; they are not quite in Miss Sitwell's new voice, and the few lines it contains in her old voice are ill at ease in this traditional company. Yet "Prelude" is of crucial importance, for it introduces the two fundamental changes in her later poetry. First, the lines have an entirely different movement. Gone are the rhythms of the Chinese wall-paper, gone the decorative details, the diminutives, the pretty Christian names, and gone, thank God, the tom-tom beats of darkness. All these have served their purpose, but they have enchanted or frightened us with a mirage; the new vision requires an ampler style, a rhythm capable of sustaining simple, passionate and prophetic statements of belief. And *Prelude* contains the first consciousness of this belief, which has been growing during these years of darkness.

> '... *the winter's shade*
> *furred my cold blood wherein plant, beast, are laid,*
> *In that dark earth from which shall spring the soul.'*

To discover Miss Sitwell's expression of this faith is not difficult; for her later poetry has the peculiarity that those ideas and images which mean most to her are constantly re-appearing in slightly different, sometimes even in identical, form. As some medieval craftsman with a store of precious jewels and antique cameos, the objects of his deepest delight, is constantly re-setting them that he may achieve absolute finality in the expression of his visionary world, so Miss Sitwell resets her most precious images. And when we find one of these re-appearing several times we may be sure that it is at the centre of her experience. Such are the closing lines of *Prelude*. They occur in almost identical language, but with the necessary modifications of prose, in the second chapter of *I Live under a Black Sun*; they re-appear again about six years later in the poem called "An Old Woman." It is significant that this last version contains lines from the prose passage which Miss Sitwell was not able to assimilate into the stricter and less assured prosodic structure of "Prelude." Clearly, this is of unusual importance to her, and I therefore quote it in full in its (till now) final form. To those interested in Miss Sitwell's technique, and in the creative process generally, I recommend a comparison of the three versions; it is a lesson in composition—although I may confess to a slight regret that 'crooked' took the place of 'cripple' in the tenth line, an improvement in texture at the expense of vividness.

61

'For when the first founts and deep waterways
Of the young light flow down and lie like peace
Upon the upturned faces of the blind
From life, it comes to bless
Eternity in its poor mortal dress—
Shining upon young lovers and old lechers
Rising from their beds, and laying gold
Alike in the unhopeful path of beggars
And in the darkness of the miser's heart.
The crooked has a shadow light made straight
The shallow places gain their strength again—
And desert hearts, waste heavens, the barren height
Forget that they are cold.
The man-made chasms between man and man
Of creeds and tongues are fill'd, the guiltless light
Remakes all men and things in holiness.'

The other key to the evolution which we are studying is the poem called "Metamorphosis." Once more the title implies consciousness that this is a poem of transition, and in fact the poem itself was to suffer a complete metamorphosis which is revealing. It was written just before "Gold Coast Customs," and is a disturbing, unfused mixture of the old Chinoiserie and the coming poetry of anguish. Both contain great beauties—indeed, Miss Sitwell's Rococo has never been more perfect than at this moment when the black wave of misery was about to engulf it. But the value of the poem lies in its other hemisphere, in the lines where death and the cold have already fastened upon the poet's mind. These are the clearest of all anticipations of her later style, and it is not surprising that when that style was mastered she should have returned to the poem and re-written it with the omission of the Rococo passages. She also omitted a few verses which perhaps she thought were sufficiently expressed in "Gold Coast Customs," but which are so magnificent in themselves that they are worth rescuing.

'I too from ruined walls hung upside down
And, bat-like, only saw Death's ruined town

62

> And mumbling, crumbling dust . . . I saw the people
> Mouthing blindly for the earth's blind nipple.
> Their thick sleep dreams not of the infinite
> Wild strength the grass must have to find the light
> With all the bulk of earth across its eyes
> And strength, and the huge weight of centuries.'

The wonderful image of the grass (which is retained in the later version) brings us very close to the beliefs from which her later poetry springs. So does the last stanza.

> 'Come then, my Sun, to melt the eternal ice
> Of Death, and crumble the thick centuries
> Nor shrink my soul, as dull wax owlish eyes
> In the sun's light, before my sad eternities.'

A comparison with the two final stanzas of the later version is like a step back from the eighteenth into the seventeenth century. The strict heroic couplets in which the first version was composed yields to a line based on rhythmic stress and not on numbered accents; the address is more passionate and more direct, and we are conscious that she has brooded on the experience of the mystics.

> 'So, out of the dark, see our great Spring begins
> —Our Christ, the new song, breaking out in the fields and
>   hedgerows,
> The heart of man! O the new temper of Christ, in veins
>   and branches.
> He comes, our Sun, to melt the eternal ice
> Of Death, the crusts of Time round the shrunken Soul
> Coming again in the spring of the world, clothed with the
>   scarlet coloured
> Blood of our martyrdoms—the fire of spring.'

These examples show that Miss Sitwell's later style was evolved in the ten years between "Gold Coast Customs" and 1939, and was not, as it is sometimes supposed, the result of the war. Nevertheless the catastrophe and the events which led up to it may have helped to focus more clearly her new poetic inspira-

63

tion, and in "Serenade," "Street Song" and "Still Falls the Rain," she wrote the greatest poems of the war. They succeed where others have failed, because in them she is able both to feel the tragedy and to transcend it. Like the great religious poets of the past, she has achieved the consciousness that all creation is one and is kept in motion by Love. In the expression of this consciousness she has evolved certain images. For example, Love is spoken of as the Sun or Gold, the heart of man, 'that second sun'.

'Fires on the hearth! Fires in the heavens! Fires in the
    hearts of Men!
I who was welded into bright gold in the earth by Death
Salute you! All the weight of Death in all the world
Yet does not equal Love—the great compassion
For the fallen dust and all fallen creatures, quickening
As is the Sun in the void firmament.
It shines like fire. O bright gold of the heat of the Sun
   Of Love across dark fields—burning away rough husks of
    Death
Till all is fire, and bringing all to harvest!
For as the Sun buries his hot days and rays
To ripen in earth, so the great rays of the heart
Are ripened to wisdom by Death . . .'

In such passages Miss Sitwell speaks with a startling directness and much of her recent poetry is of unexpected simplicity—for example, the beautiful third stanza of "Eurydice," the poem quoted above. But this simplicity is delusive, like the simplicity of all prophetic utterances; and two stanzas further on her imagery becomes mysterious, though no less beautiful, and, as we feel immediately, no less true to experience. In particular her image of death has taken on a new and mysterious meaning for her. It has become a source of peace and wisdom, a necessary state through which we must pass before love can be reborn; and her last volume opens with an Invocation to this once dreaded darkness. Yet it would be shallow to suppose that the desperate unhappiness of "Gold Coast Customs" has been completely overcome. The same horror, expressed with far more mastery, inspires her terri-

64

fying "Lullaby"; and "The Song of the Cold" itself is a cry of anguish, though in the end the poet feels strong enough to say:

'I will cry to the spring to give me the birds and the Serpent's
   speech
That I may weep for those who die of the cold—
The ultimate cold within the heart of man.'

For, beyond all Christian or Pagan mysteries, all planetary rotations, or transcendental philosophies, Miss Sitwell is moved by an immense tenderness of heart. It is this which gives reality to her war poems, and warmth to her sybilline speech. Of this tenderness she has achieved a perfect expression in that marvellous poem, "A Mother to her Dead Child," which is surely one of the most moving poems ever written by a woman. How easily it might have come to grief. But it is lifted far beyond sentimentality as the mother's sorrow is raised to a general pity for human misfortune. And then it is the work of a masterly technician.

Anyone writing about Miss Sitwell would be wise to avoid technical questions, for he can certainly not bring to them the knowledge and the delicacy of perception which she has shown in the introduction to her own *Selected Poems*. But it is important to stress the fact that the latter poems, which teach us and awaken our pity, are every bit as beautiful in texture as the poems which were written solely to delight. Nothing in her early work is finer in technique than "Green Flows the River of Lethe-O," where the smooth-sliding opiate texture of its opening stanza leads us with sinister delicacy to the abyss. In her adaptation of an elaborate technique of sound and imagery to simpler and more passionate expression, Miss Sitwell is at one with the symbolist poets of the last half century—Rilke, George, Blok and Yeats; and in fact her development has much in common with Yeats, the greatest of her immediate predecessors. I do not know how far he has influenced her directly, though that magnificent poem "The Poet Laments the coming of Old Age" certainly owes something to his inspiration, both in its imagery—'wisdom caught like a hare in the golden sack of the heart'—and in its rich declamatory rhythm. It is almost impossible to read the last two lines except

in an Irish accent. But there is an important distinction. Miss
Sitwell does not, like Yeats, use symbols with fixed meanings. She
has said of her poems that 'all expression is welded into an image,
not removed into a symbol that is inexact or squandered into a
metaphor'. The result is that although her poems may sometimes
be vaguer than those of a strict symbolist, they are more vivid
and more flexible, and they never become mere riddles, as are
some of the minor poems of Mallarmé.

In spite of Swinburnian and symbolist characteristics, it is
clear from her latest poems that Miss Sitwell's place in English
literature is with the religious poets of the seventeenth century.
Again and again the audacity of her sensuous images reminds us
of Crashaw; she has Traherne's rapture at created things, and
Vaughan's sense of eternity. The likeness is less due to direct influence—in fact these poets are seldom mentioned in her pages—
than to a similar poetic temperament working under similar conditions. Miss Sitwell is essentially a religious poet; that is to say,
she has experienced imaginatively, not merely intellectually, the
evil and misery of the world and has overcome that experience by
the conviction—the full, imaginative conviction—that all creation
is one under the Divine Love. In expressing this conviction she
has inevitably been led to use the symbols of Christianity and of
that old mystic poetry which it supplanted, combining them, as
Botticelli did, from a sense of their beauty and human relevance,
without the dogmatic niceties of neo-Platonism.

In her last published work "The Shadow of Cain" Christian
symbols have gained ascendancy. This craggy, mysterious philosophic poem, in which the poet looks down from a great eminence
of time, is at the furthest remove from the lyrics of the *hortus
conclusis*. The world without love, the world of absolute zero,
is split in two by some such disastrous convulsion of matter as now
hangs over our heads, and there are left two protagonists of humanity, Dives and Lazarus. The dialogue between them with
which the poem ends, is her deepest and most passionate statement of her concern with original sin.

66

'... we cry

To Dives: "You are the shadow of Cain. Your shade is the
    primal Hunger."
"I lie under what condemnations?"
"The same as Adam, the same as Cain, the same as Sodom,
    the same as Judas."
And the fires of your Hell shall not be quenched by the rain
From those torn and parti-coloured garments of Christ,
    those rags
That once were Men. Each wound, each stripe,
Cries out more loudly than the voice of Cain—
Saying "Am I my brother's keeper?"

This is the true cry of our time, the cry of all those whose imaginations are still awake and whose hearts are still uncalcined. Miss
Sitwell is a religious poet because only thus could she continue to
write for this generation without being overcome by despair. She
is growing in power and confidence, so that we wait thirstily for
each new poem, which, by its beauty, its compassion and its belief
in the eternal processes of recreation, can help us to endure the
world's fever.

Gordon Bottomley

This Symposium must inevitably testify to Edith Sitwell's originality, her vitality, her salient presence and immediacy in the contemporary scene; yet it is to be doubted if she ever sought originality, or thought of being anything except herself. Every writer feels to be contemporary when he takes his pen—even if it is to write about Troy or Eldorado; but those who can convince their fellows of it are contemporary by reason of their timelessness, as Miss Sitwell is. An art-critic eminent at the turn of the century was asked who was the greatest painter of all time: he replied that he did not know, but that he believed Titian to be the central one. Something of such a "central" quality is Miss Sitwell's.

It is natural that this daughter of an ancient line should, from such a position, look backward as well as forward; for when English poetry, by the union of several sources, took its eventual authentic form, it did so at the hands of the aristocracy. The young men who decided the essential forms of English verse on the lines of verse-forms already fixed in France and Italy were the young courtiers—peers and knights and members of embassies— who passed between England and the continent in the reigns of the Tudor princes; as their fore-runner Chaucer had arrived at the normal English iambic line in the company of Petrarca and Boccaccio, three courtiers together.

Poetry is not necessarily verse: every well-read man can recall the magnificent passages composed in prose. In the same way, a famous dance-band leader of to-day has pointed out that the modern dance is based on the walk. Nevertheless, Karsavina no less than Taglioni, did more than walk; and the poetic tension can develop power by the acceptance of verse-form, with its patterned rhythm that can heighten tension upon initial tension.

The wide use of *Laissez-faire* in rhythm today has tended to fix and define poetic effect while giving the poet a desired freedom: there is neither freedom nor bondage when poetry is attained. Poetry is a state of perfection in which there is no degree: "As it makes wing it gets power" wrote Wither long ago—and we watch it doing so: when the state is reached, an insatiable appetite for essential (not merely significant) form has been satisfied. It is one of Miss Sitwell's sources of poetic strength that she controls such varied means to this approach. Her sensitive notation of metrical effect is a visible testimony to her technical perception, and her means to beauty, alike: to hear her give vocal expression to her work is to understand that she composes in sound, and escapes the tyranny of the poet's ill-advised eyes fixed upon the poet's pen: "Lily O'Grady" that "lazy lady" dances toward us like Boticelli's Spring when its author reads it aloud, irresistible though

> Pompey's dead, Homer's read,
> Heliogabalus lost his head,
> And shade is on the brightest wing,
> And dust forbids the bird to sing.

The poem dances, its lines sway like dancers' draperies on a Greek vase: it is the essence of Miss Sitwell's early work, of that season of "firstness" when poetry has a bloom on it which is an enchantment—and which must be foregone for the greater things. The transition has been inevitable for her—perhaps even easy: her world of bright imagination was piquant with young perception, ironic, glittering as though with flashing dragonflies, quick with new sound—her luminous, luminant words seeming to be made at the moment, and used for the first time: and yet they sing of the State in which Alph the sacred river ran past Coleridge; where at our backs we always hear Time's winged chariot hurrying near:

where Crashaw's St. Teresa listened to his devotion; and between the wash of the tumbling seas William Morris heard Lady Alice and Lady Louise sing: although, with all this in her too, the spirit of the *scherzo* will also insist

> *And tries to cozen*
> *Them 'Buy angels' eggs*
> *Sold by the dozen' . . .*

Yet on a near-by page she can recognize "that only

> *Winged ones know the highest eyrie is so lonely.*

And in the same poem she continues

> *I always was a little outside life,—*
> *And so the things we touch could comfort me;*
> *I loved the shy dreams we could hear and see—*
> *For I was like one dead, like a small ghost,*
> *A little cold air wandering and lost.*

Which brings to mind a dedication to her in her brother's *Poems*

> *To you, sad child upon the darkened stair,*
> *Poor flaxen foundling of the upper air. . . .*
> *In you th' existence of an inner shrine*
> *Where burnt a flame most rare. . . .*

Miss Sitwell has said "In the past, with the exception of 'Goblin Market' there has been no technically sufficient poem written by a woman": but she herself has the same sense of texture, and of the shaping of rhymes and rhythms; along with the supple pliant energy—as of a springing tree—which the lowered vitality of the unfinished nun rarely compassed and soon lost. (And here it should be recognised that the Sitwells are a third family triad of genius, which the end of the 19th century added to the two which the beginning had brought—the Brontes and the Rossettis: and that of these the Brontes and the Sitwells are native to Yorkshire—while it has been stated that the one strain of English blood in the Rossettis came from the same county).

While fantasy and life were thus dancing together before her, they were not all that she noticed. A fantasy which she found in Aubrey's *Miscellanies* turned to a new gravity in her: a bereaved husband, musing on his dream of his dead wife, says

> Sun of my life, she went to warm the dead
> And I must now go sunless in their stead. . . .
> So walks a dead man, waning, in my dress,
> By black, disastrous suns of death grown less, . . .
> How shall I bear my heart without its beat, . . .
> More cold than she is in her grave's long night,
> That hath my heart for covering, warmth and light.
> But when she had been twelve months in her grave
> She came where I lay in my bed: she gave
> Her kiss. And oh, her lips were warm to me. . . .
> I stole her kiss, the only light
> She had to warm her eternal night.

And there is a further manifestation of this new gravity and ardent reflectiveness in the fragment of a tragedy on the Greek model, dealing with Saul's murder of his brother. It remains broken and unique in Miss Sitwell's *oeuvre*; although there is in it every sign of a mounting sense of form, that was even then equal to carrying it out: and there is more than an indication of the strength and vision that has since become hers in a scene between Saul's mother and another woman, elderly and dying:

> Amasa
> Nay, sit a little, warming in the sun;
> We have such withered hands that soon grow cold.
> I bore men too, and then the old grey men,
> The old grey hungry men said one word "war"—
> And wrung my children's bodies dry of blood
> And hid them in a hole lest I should kiss them,
> We are so old we should be gone,—too old
> To die, too weak to creep into the grave,
> Two poor old women: for these strong young men
> Have taken all the grave-room, and we're left!

71

This was not written in 1940; but twenty years earlier. The masterpiece of all Miss Sitwell's earlier work, her "Elegy on Dead Fashion", though rooted in the gayest parterre of her fantastic garden—flowery with cashmere pelerines, pelisses of tissue, crinolines of plaided sarsenet, velours confections, velvet bonnets for wood-nymphs, roses and cherries and strawberries bobbing at their lips like scarlet fire—suffers a forest change: the wood-nymphs in their *robes d'artifice* are pensive no more, but grave: they have forgotten their fetes and their poets—even De Musset. The sultry glades are chilled: there are austere contours within the gauzes, the veils reveal a mournful grandeur:

> *How old is Venus? older than the trees,*
> *Does she remember still the ancient bliss,*
> *Grown dead and rotten, of Adonis' kiss? . . .*
> *The nymphs are dead. And yet when Spring begins*
> *The nation of the dead must feel old sins*
> *Wake unremembering bones, eternal, old*
> *As Death. Oh, think how these must feel the cold*
> *In the deep groves! But here these dead still walk*
> *As though they lived and sigh awhile, and talk.*
> *O perfumed nosegay brought for noseless Death!*
> *My glittering fire has turned into a ghost,*
> *My rose is now cold amber and is lost. . . .*
> *DEBOUT LES MORTS! No key when the heart closes:*
> *The nymphs are dead like the great summer roses*
> *Rich as a tomb each dress! oh, pity these!*
> *Come not, O solemn and revengeful Dead,—*
> *Most loving Dead, from your eternal bed*
> *To meet this living ghost, lest you should keep*
> *Some memory of what I was, and weep.*

"Rich as a tomb each dress!" So much is over: the poet's stage is set: she comes into her kingdom, but it is afternoon, and the sun is murky behind congested smouldering clouds of war. There is no transition between "I too sit apart. . . . Knowing not goddess's from beggars' bones"; and the "Love my heart for an hour, but my bone for a day" of *Street Songs*; and the "I who had feared

72

to see That eternal truth the Bone Laid bare by Death—cried now "Come home. . . . How shall I bear my heart without its beat. . . ." of *Green Song.* . . .

Miss Sitwell had found her range—and ranged as she pleased. She took up for a moment the current fashion of illuminating one's poem with someone else's jewel; but it was her light that revealed and outshone Marlowe's in "Then die with me and be my love", which stabs like the incendiary flashes of the nights when it was written. She will free her verse with speech rhythms because her words share the life of her dancing rhythms.

Now she no longer speaks for the bright ladies in their veils and Balmoral gowns, but for all women, and those beyond fashions most of all. In her later works, more than ever, she looks into herself, and to her own apprehensions of external and internal life, for her themes. In her own phrase "The heat of the earth and beat of the heart are one."

This is indeed so, in *Green Song;* everywhere in its most notable pages the beat of the heart is apprehended, pervasive, extended to external nature, giving a subjective quality to objective things—with implications of far-reaching and searching mystic sensibility.

This latter facet of this poetry has the movement of rising flame; and a deep lucidity, that calls to mind some image of an Eastern divinity, in solid crystal, through which can be seen light alone, and not material things; and at another time an incandescence that is at the heart of flame—yet an incandescence of the spirit that must speak in symbols. Miss Sitwell's symbols are constants—the Lion and his Lioness; and all golden things, armour, women, corn; and green things that share with golden things the essence of life, which comes from the golden sun—but also the opposites of these things, that are of the lifeless light of the moon, the Skeleton, and its black covering, the final bone that is the fundament of human nature. And of mortality's divinities, too: it is of Venus and mortal perfection that she writes

> even her bone can no more stand upright
> But leans as if it thirsted—

The bone has as heart-disturbing an influence on her apprehension as it had on Donne's—

> That eternal truth the Bone
> Laid bare by Death—
> > the poor Dead for whom the Spring
> Is cold . . .

And my love, that white lady, is but a thin white bone. Even Venus, "that was the world's desire" (in the piece which may be thought the most mind-searching of these impressive poems) when

> the first soundless wrinkles fall like snow
> On many a golden cheek,
> > knows the anguish of the bone
> Deserted by all love.

But

> The old unchanging memory of the bone—
> That porphyry whence grew the Summer rose,
> > teaching the dust that it is holy,

carries the pervasive promise of these Green Songs, of renewal, "And Death the pain of earth turning to Spring again": the Summer roses that

> care not for our philosophies
> Of life and death, knowing the earth's forgiveness.

That "thin white bone" is sometimes something connected with night and seen in its thin white light which is moonlight. But moonlight's source is sunlight—left behind by

> the Abraham-bearded Sun, the father of all things
> . . . shouting of ripeness over our harvest—
> The Sun Whose Body was spilt on our fields to bring us
> > harvest,
> > the ear of wheat to the Lost Men
> Who asks the city stones if they are bread,
> > the crumb
> For the starving bird

74

that is

> part of the broken Body
> of Christ Who forgives us—He with the bright Hair
> —The Sun Whose Body was spilt on our fields to bring us
> harvest.

From poem to poem these musical themes transmit themselves, transforming in new surroundings while maintaining a ground-bass of consciousness of the poet's unresting purpose, her apprehensions of the life of the spirit in the body of man and earth alike.

Some quotations must be given if anything like an adequate depiction of this illuminating and illuminated book is to be given. "Invocation" is "for a rebirth of faith and of wonder," "when spring begins to the sound of the heart and the planetary rhythm";

> For a darker rain to cool the delirium of gold
> And wash the sore of the world,

against

> The gossips of mean Death . . .
> The small and gilded scholars of the Fly
> That feed upon the crowds and their dead breath
> And buzz and stink where the bright heroes die . . .

An Invocation, also, to light, that

> Tells to that little child the humble dust
> Tales of the old world's holiness;

and to Love, to

> return to the dying world, as the light
> Of morning, shining in all regions, latitudes
> And households of high heaven in the heart,

and to primal Law, to

> Rule then the spirit working in dark earth
> As the Sun and Planets rule the husbandman.

And when the night of the world falls, an Invocation to the "Spirit moving upon the waters" to

> Bring peace to the famine of the heart and lips—

to

> Be then the sleep
> When Judas gives again the childish kiss
> That once his mother knew.

In contrast from that dead mother whose child had lived we turn to that other invocation, "A Mother To Her Dead Child," whose hands, "push back the dark" that "is its nurse": an invocation to

> Return from your new mother
> The earth: she is too old for your little body,
> Too old for the small tendernesses, the kissings . . .
>   forgetting

> That children are restless like the small spring shadows:
and neither "the huge pangs of winter," nor "the spring's birth" will

> lay your heart bare to my heart again
> In your small earthly dress.

Miss Sitwell writes, in her finest lyric that would be worthy of Donne's daughter or Crashaw's sister:

> Said the Lion to the Lioness, 'When you are amber dust . . .
> Remember still the flowering of the amber blood and bone,
> The rippling of bright muscles like a sea,
> Remember the rose-prickles of bright paws
> Though we shall mate no more
> Till the fire of that sun the heart and the moon-cold bone
>   are one.'

And again

76

Said the Sun to the Moon—'When you are but a lonely
    white crone,
And I, a dead king in my golden armour somewhere in a
    dark wood,
Remember only this of our hopeless love
That never till Time is done
Will the *fire* of the heart and the *fire* of the mind be one.'

Yet when the mother holds her dead child in her breast while
she can still speak to it, Time *is* done, and the heart and mind sink
into one in the dying fires.

EDITH SITWELL: *Text of a Broadcast delivered over the German Service of the B.B.C.*

John Lehmann

In every country of Europe, where the war-storm has passed, one of the most haunting sights today is that of the ruined churches and cathedrals. Splendid monuments of Gothic and Baroque stand open to the weather, with fallen towers and broken pillars, and where the jewels of stained glass patterning once caught the sunlight is now a gaping emptiness. Some of these great churches are very ancient indeed, and are built round the remains of Roman or Graeco-Roman temples, which the battering they have so recently endured has revealed in the midst of the accretions of later ages. These ruins dominate the landscape, symbols of three thousand years of our civilization and the tragic face it wears today; and yet, when—as sometimes happens—services are held among the ruins, and candles are lit on the altars and the fountain of singing rises again into the air, life and hope seem to wake again and the shattered arches to be transfigured with a promise of restoration and continuity.

This may seem to you to have very little to do with modern poetry; and yet in reading the work of Edith Sitwell such images have constantly entered my mind. Among all modern poets she seems to me to be supreme in seeing the tragedy of our age in the perspective not only of all the history and all the thought and art that began for us so long ago in the lands of the Eastern Mediterranean, but also of the undateable antiquity of the universe beyond that. So that you can have some idea at once of the quality of her work, I would like you to hear one of the most beautiful poems she wrote during the war,—remembering, of course, that even the best translation can only convey part of the beauty of so subtle a poet. It is called "Heart and Mind."*

The first thing that must strike anyone who hears these lines, is the extraordinary mastery of the poet who wrote them over the music and texture of verse—the fineness of her ear,—and the beautiful effects she achieves by her handling of rhythm, the subtle counterpointing of her basic metrical structure. Edith Sitwell did not suddenly reveal this mastery out of nothing. It is the result of a long and devoted apprenticeship to her art. When her first books appeared, a quarter of a century ago, they charmed and surprised the reading public by their freshness of vision, the bold association of images, the fluency of the music. Some people, who could not disentangle themselves from traditional assumptions—from what they had been taught to expect poetry to be— were completely bewildered by these poems which had the innocence and inconsequence of nursery rhymes, in which sense-impressions were all jumbled up so that light was said to 'creak' and fire to be 'furry as a bear'. These poems are nonsense, the disbelievers said. . . . And perhaps they were right without knowing it, for nonsense can also be that kind of evocative nonsense out of which Shakespeare created some of the most wonderful songs in his plays, which will last much longer than many another poem with an elaborate logical precision of meaning. These poems are frivolous, the disbelievers also said. . . . . But there they were wrong. Edith Sitwell was always serious about her poetry, as serious as an artist with a deep sense of vocation can be. She was intensely serious then in her attempt to create a new kind of beauty, of imaginative life, out of the marriage of symbols that nobody had brought together before her. She is intensely serious now in something that to me is of far greater significance and power, but could probably never have been achieved without those daring exercises at the bar, that developed the suppleness of her poetic limbs in so remarkable a fashion.

---

*This poem appears on page 144.

The early poetry of Edith Sitwell is the poetry of an enchanted garden. It was with "Gold Coast Customs," written a year or two before the war, that a change began to come over her work: the outer world, with all its sufferings and struggle, had broken into the enchanted garden, and the result was a long poem, of almost savage metrical force, as insistent as a tom-tom, which purporting to describe native African customs, was in reality a macabre satire on a world where the rich and powerful seemed to have no mercy for the weak and innocent. To read this poem was to realise that Edith Sitwell had brooded long and deeply on human misery, to see with sudden illumination how deep the wounds were which the sufferings of others had made in her heart. The full harvest, however, was still to come. It was in the middle of the war that *Street Songs* appeared, a volume that announced with unmistakable assurance, that Edith Sitwell had advanced from being a poet who created a fascinating personal world with unique technical virtuosity, to become an inspired voice that spoke for all the spiritual distress and longing of an agonised generation, with a dignity, a compassion, a breadth of vision and an artistic maturity that only the masters of European poetry can command. *Street Songs* was followed by *Green Song*, in which she displayed her new 'grand manner' in further, astonishing variations. You have heard the first poem in this book "Heart and Mind." You may have felt that the sufferings of modern Europe were very far away from such writing. But Edith Sitwell is a symbolist, and though she never actually mentions the war,—the campaigns, the air-raids, the shattered homes and maimed families,—it is there behind her symbols all the time, and it is her vision of its drama that informs her whole utterance. Sometimes she comes much closer to direct comment. Here is another poem from "Green Song," one of the most beautiful, called "Invocation":

> *I who was once a golden woman like those who walk*
> *In the dark heavens—but am now grown old*
> *And sit by the fire, and see the fire grow cold,*
> *Watch the dark fields for a rebirth of faith and wonder.*

The turning of Ixion's wheel the day
Ceased not, yet sounds no more the beat of the heart
But only the sound of ultimate darkness falling
And of the Blind Samson at the Fair, shaking the pillars of
*   the world and emptily calling.*

For the gardeners cried for rain, but the high priests howled
For a darker rain to cool the delirium of gold
And wash the sore of the world, the heart of Dives,
Raise wheat for the hunger that lies in the soul of the poor—
Then came the thunderous darkness. . . .

You will notice that Edith Sitwell takes symbols from the widest range within our common culture, from Classical and Christian legend and history, and even beyond, from the primitive pre-history and shadowy beliefs of Europe; and she marries them with the more ancient and universal symbols of animal and flower, sea and sun and stars. It is by such means that she manages to convey, in her supreme poems, such an extraordinary sense of depth in Time and Space, of wisdom ripening in eternal contemplation from a mountain-top vantage point. And what meaning has this vision, this wisdom for us? In such rich and complex poetry, it is dangerous to define any pattern too precisely: there will always be more in the poetry than can be elucidated in mere prose analysis. But the heart, I believe, of Edith Sitwell's philosophy is the quite simple idea,—simple, yet so often lost sight of, and seldom so beautifully expressed,—that as the world of nature is transformed and restored again and again by the creative action of the sun, so Love transforms and conquers all our sufferings, all the passing triumphs of evil, so that 'all in the end is harvest'. Listen to "Eurydice," to this triumphal chant rising from the ruined church that was once a temple and is now open to the stars:

Fire on the hearth! Fire in the heavens! Fire in the hearts
*   of men!*
I who was welded into bright gold in the earth by Death
Salute you! All the weight of Death in all the world

81

Yet does not equal Love—the great compassion
For the fallen dust and all fallen creatures, quickening
As is the Sun to the void firmament.
It shines like fire, O bright gold of the heat of the Sun
Of Love across dark fields—burning away rough husks of
        Death
Till all is fire, and bringing all to harvest!

A NOTE ON EDITH SITWELL'S POETRY

Arthur Waley

"The Way that can be told is not the Eternal Way", says Lao Tzu, and the same is true of Poetry. Critics today try to get round this by treating poetry as a social product and showing the connection between the poet and his material surroundings. This is fun for the critic, who enjoys knocking the mystery-man off his perch and making him line up for once in the common queue, and it is not at all uninteresting for the reader. But it is sociology, not poetics, and though the poet is perfectly fair game for the sociologist, the sort of thing this method tells one would apply just as much to bad poets as to good. The psychological method, which might at first seem to be more applicable, lets us down in just the same way. It throws no light on quality. It can show just how Shakespeare's Oedipus-complex is reflected in *Hamlet*: it cannot explain why other dramatists' Oedipus-complex did not lead to equally good results.

Theoretically, discussions about the poet's mythology and technique are open to the same objection. In practice, however, it does not work out quite that way. Take, for example, Miss Edith Sitwell's poetry. Technique is of course only a vehicle; it is not poetry itself any more than a perambulator is a baby. But I do not know any instance of a bad poet having technical skill at all comparable to that of Miss Sitwell, and although the enormously wide range of her subject-matter could not by itself make her a good poet, I think one may at least say that the skimpy range

83

of the Georgian Nature Poets (who held the field when she began to write) made it unlikely that they would produce anything but a crude and over-simplified form of poetry.

That is why I have chosen in this note chiefly to discuss her technique and material, fully aware that in doing so I am merely skirting the periphery of her art.

She herself has written very fully about one aspect of technique—the deliberate choice of words not merely for their meaning but also for the emotional effect of their sound. For example, of a poem that expresses the furry, growling, bear-like quality of primitive nature she says: "It is built on a scheme of harsh 'r's'," and shows just how. She has indeed, as regards her own verse, gone into this subject so thoroughly in the preface to her *Selected Poems* (1936), that there is no need to discuss it here. Metrically, she has on the whole been traditional. She has never written the sort of free-verse which uses prose rhythm and is indeed merely prose printed as though it were poetry. On the rare occasions when she altogether discards rhyme she uses the ordinary blank-verse line (as in that very beautiful early fragment, "The Madness of Saul") or something fairly close to it. Her usual forms have till recently been the traditional four-stress or five-stress lines of standard English poetry, with latterly a tendency to six-stress lines such as

I who was once a golden woman like those who walk . . .

In the most recent poems ("Eurydice", for example) many seven and eight-stress lines occur and the versification has become much looser. Lines sometimes have a recitative cadence and even assume the dimensions of small paragraphs, as in "Green Song".

With the bird-notes of Doom in the egg, and Fate in the bud that is flushed with the world's fever.

This is, of course, an eight-stress line, and the use of such lines gives scope for immense variety of cadence, created by different distributions of the pauses. I think that the ear, used to shorter divisions, takes a little time to accommodate itself to these sustained periods. It is too, so far as I have noticed, only since about

84

1940 that Miss Sitwell has taken to using Sprung Rhythm, one feature of which is to allow two fully stressed syllables to stand side by side, without an intervening light-syllable or syllables to buffer them, as in the poem from *Street Song* called "Tears":

The rocks of great diamonds in the midst of the clear wave,

which occurs in a scheme of six-stress lines. Or again in "Most Lovely Shade":

Deep in the dark secret of the rose.

This is of course quite a different thing from the distribution of a stress over two syllables, as in the line from "The Peach Tree":

Until your long dark fluid hands unfold

where the stress is shared by "long" and "dark," each getting half of it.

Slightly apart, in Miss Sitwell's metrical development, stand a few early poems that were evoked by popular tunes. "Polka," for example, is a libretto rather than a poem:

'Tra la la la—
See me dance the polka;
Said Mr. Wagg like a bear,
'With my top hat
And my whiskers that—
(Tra la la) trap the Fair.'

I have only quoted the opening lines. One has to read them to a polka tune, and that deprives them of complete independence as poetry. But the commonly held idea that all the poems subsequently set to music by William Walton in *Facade* were inspired by music or (alternatively) were written to be set to music is quite false. Nothing, for example, could be more a poem in its own right than "Sylph's Song"—the one which begins:

Daisy and Lily
Lazy and silly
Walk by the shore of the wan grassy sea . . .

There has been a lot of trouble about Miss Sitwell's use of metaphor and simile. One can best explain this by saying that it is the opposite of Dante's. Dante looks for the likest possible concrete parallel. The graves of the sectaries in Hell are like the graves outside Arles; the hoods worn by the hypocrites are like those worn by the monks at Cologne (and if you don't happen to have been to Arles or Cologne, Dante seems to say, there's nothing to be done about it). Sometimes he stays so close to what he is illustrating that he seems almost to be going in circles, as when he says that what he felt on hearing Beatrice's voice was like what Pyramus felt when he heard Thisbe's. If one had asked Dante, "And what *did* Pyramus feel?", he would presumably have had to answer, "Just what *I* felt", and so left us just where we started. Miss Sitwell, on the contrary, always gets far enough away from her starting-point to make sure that her metaphor or image throws light on her subject from a new angle. No one today is likely to quarrel with her (as they did in the twenties) for making cross cuts from one sense to another (calling light "shrill" or the like). "Where the language of one sense is insufficient", she has told us, "to convey a meaning, a sensation, I use another, and by this means I attempt to pierce down to the essence of the thing seen". When she says in "Metamorphosis"

> I looked out from my window where the urban
> Leaves seemed turkeys, (Sultans in a turban),
> Across the lake where, cupolas and gables,
> The ripples seemed deserted Georgian stables ...

one is perfectly satisfied by the ripples-stables image. The motion of the water pulls its flatness into arcs and curves, just as the prevailing straightness of Georgian line is broken by cupola and gable. But I think something else happens too. The strangeness of the comparison, its apparent remoteness from the thing imaged, acts like a sudden, sharp rap on the table of the senses and startles them into vivid apprehension. Sometimes, however, when the poet does not aim at sudden illumination, her images and allusions are gently led up to, somewhat as the musician "prepares" a modulation. Thus near the beginning of "The Sleeping Beauty"

86

the mention of Fortunatus, who according to Medieval legend had a purse that never ran dry, leads up to the "Figs, each like a purse of gold"; further on, the mention of the Mikado prepares us for the likening of the spell-bound Dowager-queen to the arrested wave on a screen by the Japanese painter Korin. If Miss Sitwell's poetry were a network of such allusions it would be uphill work for the average modern reader. But it is not. They are only occasional, and the classical references (which are by far the most numerous) are of an everyday kind. Daphne, Corydon, Amaryllis, Philomel, Proserpine are not recondite figures, and the reader to whom they are unfamiliar can easily find out about them (as presumably Miss Sitwell had to do herself).

When *Street Songs* appeared in 1942 immense surprise and gratification were expressed at the fact that Miss Sitwell had noticed the war, mobilized herself and written poems about the air-raids. Reviewers wrote as though she had hitherto dealt only with an enchanted world, half-nursery, half Mont Parnasse, had shut herself away behind the 'gilded trellises' of wit and phantasy. This was of course a strange line to take about some one who had written long ago such humanly tragic poems as "Metamorphosis", "The Hambone and the Heart", "The Lament of Edward Blastock" and "Gold Coast Customs", three of which poems (or considerable parts of them) were included by W. B. Yeats in the *Oxford Book of Modern Verse* (1936), and were therefore particularly accessible. But the new enthusiasm was certainly not misplaced. "Still Falls the Rain", "Lullaby", "The Youth with the Red-gold Hair", "The Night Before Great Babylon", "The Swans" (all from *Street Songs*) are some of the finest poems that Miss Sitwell has written. Where I think she is not completely successful is in some of the recent poems about Death. The material she uses is too restricted and too imperfectly mythologized. Think for a moment of the wealth of allusion, of the constant changes of atmosphere—classical, contemporary, Spanish, fairy-tale, Georgian—in her poems of Life, contrasted with her narrow world of Death, in which the denizens do not even seem (like Emily Dickinson's dead) to "Talk between the rooms", but appear to be locked away each in a private skeletal anguish. Personally I am inclined to agree with the maxim in Hilaire Belloc's nonsense-rhyme:

> There is a good deal to be said
> For being dead,

and am much more sorry for the living. That, however, is only a difference of opinion and not a criticism of Miss Sitwell's Death poems. But I do think that the comparative poverty of her Death mythology has definitely had a handicapping effect on many of her recent poems, making as it does for a too frequent repetition of the same words and images. Recently Miss Sitwell, as though she too felt that she needed the help of an accepted mythology for her Death poems, has used the story of Orpheus and Eurydice. It is a poem that begins magnificently:

> Fires on the hearth! Fires in the heavens! Fires in the
> hearts of Men!

But I feel that the references to Proserpina, Osiris and Adonis work as ethnological parallels rather than as flowerings of the Orpheus myth itself. Moreover the name of Proserpina is bound up in one's mind with the very sensible arrangement that was ultimately made about her: she was to spend the winter in Hades and the summer on Earth, a compromise by which we still benefit. Miss Sitwell leaves her tragically lying "in the silent Tomb"— where after all she was having an affair with her winter-husband, Pluto. For these and other reasons I do not feel that the mythology is integrated into the poem so successfully as, for example, in the early poem about Apollo and Daphne, that begins:

> Heat of the sun that maketh all men black,—
> They are but Ethiopian shades of thee—
> Pour down upon this wild and glittering fleece
> That is more rich than feathers of bright birds,
> The ripening gems, the drops of the still night.

And here I must apologize for quoting so little of Miss Sitwell's poetry. But this is a note of her methods, not an anthology.

So I cannot give whole poems, and she does not deal in "good lines" (any more than music does in "good bars") not even in "fine passages." Everything fits into everything else and every value depends on its ambience. As though to prove this Miss Sitwell once took the lines:

> Beautiful carriages from Champs Elysée
> Filled with maidens on cushions easy

which had been quoted to her as a specimen of the "worst poetry ever written" (they are attributed to a lady called Georgina Farrer) and embedded them, with full acknowledgements, in her poem "Lady Immoraline" where, provided with suitable surroundings, they cut a very reputable figure.

MISS SITWELL'S POETRY

Charles Morgan

During the last five years no artist has so remarkably increased in stature as Miss Edith Sitwell. To read the present volume, which, though a few earlier verses are included in it, is broadly representative of her work during that period is to be a witness of an astonishing metamorphosis.

There was a time when the provocative playboys claimed her as their own, and she gave colour to their claim. To the discerning it was evident that she was distinct from them, as a horse of breeding, however high-spirited its behaviour now and then, is distinct from a herd of donkeys dressed for the fair and kicking up their heels. She had always a piercing imagination and a wealth of language which the playboys could not imitate; she was fertile, they were barren; she was genuinely experimenting—that is to say, was listening, amid the babel of fashionable defiances, for the voice of her own muse—and they were kicking up their heels to make a cloud of dust. The distinction is now clear; these poems establish it; but it has not always been clear in the public mind, or even in the minds of those whom Alice Meynell spoke of as "The Little Nation", and it is necessary to emphasize it.

*   *   *

How did the confusion arise? Not, I think, from any doubt at any time of Miss Sitwell's being a true poet, but from a doubt whether the gold would emerge from the dross, the style from the mannerism; and for this doubt Miss Sitwell herself was in part

90

responsible. She trailed her coat. Two things remained unproved: first, that she was capable of those great acceptances without which, in our age of darkness, poetry is not poetry but a screaming in the dark; secondly, that, in so far as she was unaccepting, she was that great thing—a timeless challenger, and not that petty thing—a yapping rebel. These two things are proved now. The glory of her book rests upon the proof.

> *I who was once a golden woman like those who walk*
> *In the dark heavens—but am now grown old*
> *And sit by the fire, and see the fire grow cold,*
> *Watch the dark fields for a rebirth of faith and wonder.*

It is of this rebirth that now stirs in the poet herself, possessing her imagination. She has transcended the angry vanities of our dying materialism. She sees, and has learned to accept, what has befallen us, not as a disaster to be averted by contrivances, but as an event less mechanical, an event in harmony with the nature of things, a new Fall presaging redemption, a veritable Death or Winter of Man presaging a new birth in faith and wonder.

*   *   *

Not presaging it only but profoundly accomplishing it. Winter is not only Spring's forerunner but, with Spring, a necessary part of the eternal cycle:

> *So we, ruled by those laws, see their fulfilment.*
> *And I who stood in the grave-clothes of my flesh*
> *Unutterably spotted with the world's woes*
> *Cry, "I am Fire. See, I am the bright gold . . .*
> *Returning to darkness—I am fecundity, harvest."*

Death, in one of Miss Sitwell's new poems "Eurydice," is seen, not as a negation, but as being, with winter, a means to ripeness,

> *For as the Sun buries his hot days and rays*
> *To ripen in earth, so the great rays of the heart*
> *Are ripened to wisdom by Death, and great is our*
>   *forgiveness.*

And the magnificent conclusion of "Harvest" joins the Christian

91

with the natural metaphor in pursuit of the same theme. I shall
not quote it but shall be content with the passage immediately
preceding it. The poet has been speaking of the Risen Mercy for

> the wise and the foolish
> Who like the rose care not for our philosophies
> Of life and death, knowing the earth's forgiveness
> And the great dews that come to the sick rose:
> For those—

And here are lines to take the breath away—

> For those who build great mornings for the world
> From Edens of lost sight seen in each other's eyes
> Yet soon must wear no more the light of the Sun,
> But say farewell among the morning sorrows.

"From Edens of lost sight seen in each other's eyes"—that is
what the playboys could never have written! That is what has
come to Miss Sitwell, attentive to the voice of her own Muse, upon
an unchanted echo which, unlike the echoes or quotations from
Marlowe or from Rimbaud, which she deliberately uses, we seem
to recognise but cannot name. Great poetry is always full of these
deep, remote echoes; they are its heredity, its proof of breeding,
giving to what is new a miraculous maturity. If poetry does not,
in this way, summon for the reader its ancestral ghosts, if it appears
to him raw and unrooted, then—unless the fault be in his blindness or deafness—the poetry itself it wanting; and there is no more
persuasive evidence that Miss Sitwell's later poetry has power to
endure than the sense of age that its newness gives.

*　　*　　*

It is because "Gold Coast Customs," a long poem of an earlier period, brilliant though it is in colour and impact, does not respond to this test that it seems not only to belong to a different
category of verse from the fully mature work but to be, in all respects, inferior to it. It is alive; I feel its force and pressure; but, its

92

life is that of an automaton; it springs from nothing and generates nothing. Listen.

> Where flaps degraded
> The black and sated
> Slack macerated
> And antiquated
> Beckoning negress
> Nun of the shade.
> And the rickety houses
> Rock and rot,
> Lady Bamburgher airs
> That foul plague-spot
> Her romantic heart.
> From the cannibal-mart,
> That smart Plague-cart,
> Lady Bamburgher rolls where the foul news-sheet
> And the shambles for souls are set in the street.

This, it may be said, is a preliminary statement of the Chaos to be transcended, of "the long hunt for Nothing" still fiercely pursued. Even so, it is raw; it has not been assimilated in poetry. The play-boys, if they had been clever enough, might conceivably have written it, but only the poet regenerate, only a poet of faith and wonder whose originality welled up from the tradition could have written—

> Now falls the night of the world:—O spirit moving upon the
>   waters
> Your peace instil
> In the animal heat and splendour of the blood
> Bring peace to the famine of the heart and lips,
> And to the Last Man's loneliness
> Of those who dream they can bring back sight to the blind!
> You are the Night
> When the long hunt for Nothing is at rest
> In the Blind Man's Street, and in the human breast
> The hammer of Chaos is stilled.

Consider, finally, these lines of supreme tenderness—in which the charities of the human heart are infused by a divine compassion that only the highest poetry can receive into itself:

> Be then the sleep
> When Judas gives again the childish kiss
> That once his mother knew—and wash the stain
> From the darkened hands of the universal Cain.

"From Edens of lost sight . . ." "Be then the sleep . . ." The poet of these lines, of this formidable and profound volume, has heard the ultimate music and has the instrument to interpret it. What is she to Lady Bamburgher or Lady Bamburgher to her?

EDITH SITWELL

Richard Church

This is a fellow practitioner looking at Edith Sitwell's work. And a fellow-practitioner is always at a disadvantage as a critic, because he is forced to look out from behind the massive back of his own demon; that obstinate monitor who makes his life a purgatory, crashing into his privacy of soul, his friendships, his very admirations and enjoyments of other people's personalities and works.

For this reason I came late to an enjoyment of Edith Sitwell's poetry. I first met it a quarter of a century ago, sitting one day in the rooms of W. H. Davies, who showed me a poem by her and told me how she and her two brothers had recently launched into the literary life. I looked at the poem, as I looked subsequently at volume after volume, and I was blind. I was as obstinate as that greedy monitor,—that demon whom I must call my own creative urge, obliged me to be. Striving after my own way of self-expression in this strange, mad, superbly sane medium, the medium of poetry, I could not see, and would not see, the way in which this new poet was building up her own idiom. For what a new, odd, outrageous idiom it was. Either consciously or unconsciously (I am not sure even today), she was bursting asunder all the rules, and treading underfoot those fences between the arts of poety, music and painting which the great critic Lessing erected so finally in the eighteenth century.

95

In those early years of my acquaintance with Miss Sitwell's work, I saw in this contraband action only wilfulness, extravagance, a naughty desire to shock. When I heard her sing that

The gardener plays his old bagpipe
To make the melons' gold seeds ripe;
The music swoons with a sad sound—
Keep, my lad, to the safe ground!

I wanted to tell her to apply that council to herself. For I knew nothing of the significance of that image of the gardener, nor that it was the opening aspect of a very precise and ordered world, a universe that was a whole civilisation in itself, with which Miss Sitwell and her brothers were determined to express their philosophy of life; introducing as it were into the art of poetry a caste system based upon a set of values already fading out of the modern, deliquescent world of democracy. That gardener was a figure in an aristocratic sensibility; a rich, amply garnished environment of the great country-house life of England, with its deep, trailing glories from the past of family history, monumental preserves, feudal allegiances. I have since found it to be very beautiful, although it has died since those days, died rapidly of an economic collapse as the structure of Europe has come crashing down about our ears. Osbert, Miss Sitwell's brother, is raising a memorial to it in his prose autobiography; a memorial whose beauty of carving will surely arrest the passerby for many centuries to come, to muse there in a Thomas Gray-like mood, about things, habits, people, and a superb culture, all of them but dimly to be apprehended by this creature of posterity who has been touched, and stopped, by the curves and graces of Sir Osbert's paragraphs.

Yes, I have since entered into that symbolism, which Miss Sitwell announced so provocatively twenty-five years ago. I can appreciate now that the world as she saw it, and looked back upon even in those days, was one where

. . . all the beauty of the world lay deep
Mirrored within the beauty water-clear
Of flowering boughs; Helen and Dierdre dreamed

> *And fading, wakened in that loveliness*
> *Of watry branches. In that dead wild spring*
> *Through the bird's shaken voice we heard God sing.*

Oh this blind madness of our own concerns! Why did I not know, not appreciate, in those days what suffering and rapture, what exquisite feeling and divisions of thought (for thought divided is the essence of pain), were crystallised in this facade of new symbols, savage symbols, with glittering contradictions of image, tormented and telescoped out of all logical sequence; and all done out of an urgency of experience?

Even today I am not sure of the artistic justification for some of them. A poet should not shock but persuade. But why argue now about a discarded technique? One artist may be baffled, even enraged, by the way in which another artist works, but in the long run he must come to the conviction that all is justified by the accumulative results, and that continuity in a set way can be in itself a salvation, and a process of truth.

> *Who knows what beauty ripens from dark mould*
> *After the sad wind and the winter's cold?*
> *But a small wind sighed, colder than the rose*
> *Blooming in desolation, "No one knows."*

That "winter's cold", at a later time, gave me the clue to this poet's genius. And a rare genius I found it; a force working upon a family mythology, shared with the poet's brothers, weaving and weaving, intricate explorations of the special symbol, gradually fining it down to a bare statement, so bare that all the privacy of ornament was whittled away, with the poem becoming ever more universal and immediate in its application to the suffering of the general reader.

Coincident with this development of technique, the poet was devastated in all her moral, social and individual values by the break-down of European life. Everything she had cherished, not only for its own sake as the very image of her way of life as she knew it in terms of family and caste tradition, but also as it had served her through her career as an artist for a reservoir of images and symbols; all this came crashing down, and left her to "the

97

winter's cold." From a poet specializing in formal experiment, she emerged into what I am forced to call anonymity; she became a voice of the people of England, an England swept by the worst storm in its history. She was now hardly a poet with a name: she was a voice crying in the wilderness; wild, distraught in its utterance, sybilline and terrifying. She seemed to pass beyond the bounds of literary form, and to demand not criticism but recognition; and to demand where the demand was unnecessary, since the recognition was instant.

Yet, with this emergence into a prophetic stance out of the more deliberate attitude of literature, Miss Sitwell remained herself. The poetry written by her during the war passed, as it were, through the small door of recollection of those days in her early life when she first experienced "the winter's cold". Is it not significant that her war poetry should be collected up into a volume and called by her *The Song of the Cold?* Was this a warning to the reader not to insist too emphatically upon the change which had taken place in her work: a reminder that after all the new Cassandra, crying before the ruins of our latterday Troy, was still the daughter of a House which had made her, blood and spirit, during the long years of seclusion in the garden of family and privilege?

For the gardeners cried for rain, but the high priests howled
For a darker rain to cool the delirium of gold
And wash the sore of the world, the heart of Dives,
Raise wheat for the hunger that lies in the soul of the poor—
Then came the thunderous darkness
And the fly-like whispering of small hopes, small fears,
The gossips of mean Death—gadflies and gnats, the summer
    world:
The small and gilded scholars of the Fly
That feed upon the crowds and their dead breath
And buzz and stink where the bright heroes die
Of the dust's rumours and the old world's fevers.
Then fell the world in winter.

98

There is the history of what happened in that garden, and in the tradition on which that poet had founded her art. By a gigantic revolution within herself, so complete that it embraced the whole self, linking her past and present, she "sold all that she had, and gave it to the poor". She is poor herself now, poor in spirit; and therefore infinitely richer and more authoritative. By sacrificing personality, mannerism, the pride of her art, she has, by this paradox of what must be called moral action, at last full found herself; a self destitute of self, with a singing voice as much hierarchic as poetic in its authority. What gardens now she sings: no longer ornamental and peacock-trodden; but gardens of future, still too far to be seen in substance, because the world is dark about them, and the storm is still raging!

> Now falls the night of the world:—O Spirit moving upon
>   the waters
> Your peace instil
> In the animal heat and splendour of the blood—
> The hot gold of the sun that flames in the night
> And knows not down-going
> But moves with the revolutions of the heavens.
> The thunders and the fires and acclamations
> Of the leaves of spring are stilled, but in the night
> The Holy Ghost speaks in the whispering leaves.
> O wheat-ear shining like a fire and the bright gold,
> O water brought from far to the dying gardens!

Those dying gardens are the lands of Europe, with their ancient glory and history so rich and various. Note how the poet fixes upon the image of the wheat-ear. It is one of the few constants which she has kept, along with fire, water, the Sun, the Holy Ghost. She sings in a hungry world, a starving Europe, and is obsessed with the cry of the people who are left to rebuild on the ruins, and she sees "mankind's dark seed-time", and the fields where "the young women wait like the mother of corn for the lost one", and she hears everybody speaking

The universal language of the Bread—
(O Thou who art not broken, not divided—
Thou who art eaten, but like the Burning Bush
Art not consumed—Thou Bread of Men and Angels)—
The Seraphim rank on rank of the ripe wheat—
Gold-bearded thunders and hierarchies of heaven
Roar from the earth: 'Our Christ is arisen, He comes
            to give a sign from the Dead.

SITWELL EDITH SITWELL

Gertrude Stein

In a minute when they sit when they sit around her.

Mixed it with two who. One two two one two two. Mixed it with two who.

Weeks and weeks able and weeks.

No one sees the connection between Lily and Louise, but I do.

After each has had after each has had, after each has had had had it.

Change in time.

A change in time is this, if a change in time. If a change in time is this. If a change in time.

Did she come to say who.

Not to remember weeks to say and asking, not to remember weeks to-day. Not to remember weeks to say. Not to remember weeks to say and asking.

And now a bow.

When to look when to look up and around when to look down and around when to look down and around when to look around and around and altered.

Just as long as any song.

And now altogether different.

It was in place of places and it was here.

Supposing she had had a key supposing she had answered, supposing she had had to have a ball supposing she had it fall and she had answered. Supposing she had it and in please, please never see so.

As much even as that, even can be added to by in addition, listen.

Table table to be table to see table to be to see me, table to me table to be table to table to table to it. Exactly as they did it when when she was not and not and not so. After that perhaps.

She had a way of she had a way of not the name.

Little reaching it away.

As afternoon to borrow.

It made a difference.

This is most.

Introduces.

This is for her and not for Mabel Weeks.

She could not keep it out.

Introduces have and heard.

Miss Edith Sitwell have and heard.

Introduces have and had.

Miss Edith Sitwell have and had.

Introduces have and had introduces have and had and heard.

Miss Edith Sitwell have and had and heard.

Left and right.

Part two of Part one.

If she had a ball at all, if she had a ball at all too.

Fill my eyes no no.

It was and held it.

The size of my eyes.

Why does one want to or to and to, when does one want to and to went to.

To know it as well as all there.

If a little other more not so little as before, now they knew and that and so.

What in execute.

Night is different from bright.

When he was a little sweeter was he.

Part two.

There was a part one.

He did seem a little so.

Half of to mention it at all.

102

And now to allow literally if and it will if and it does if and it has if and it is.

Never as much as a way.

How does she know it.

She could be as she sleeps and as she walks all day. She could be as she sleeps and as she wakes all day is it not so.

It leads it off of that.

Please carried at.

Twice at once and carry.

She does and care to and cover and never believe in an and being narrow.

Happily say so.

What is as added.

And opposite.

Now it has to be something entirely different and it is.

Not turned around.

No one knows two two more.

Lose and share all and more.

Very easily arises.

It very easily arises.

Absently faces and by and by we agree.

By and by faces apparently we agree.

Apparently faces by and by we agree.

By and by faces apparently we agree.

Apparently faces by and by we agree.

SOME NOTES ON EDITH SITWELL

John Russell

Myself not a poet, nor even a habitual reader of poetry, I can only stand on the far boundary of this number and lob into its midst some memories of a conversation with a writer who recently died at a moment when we all had most need of his advice and example.

Logan Pearsall Smith had by his bedside a revolving ark of necessary books—one of those ugly but commodius pieces of library furniture which has four faces and spins upon a central column. The books on its shelves never varied; there were dictionaries of many kinds, glossaries of Spanish and German idioms, an Icelandic manual, some Dante lexicons, Roget in several editions, Poole's Parnassus (a 17th century manual of English poetical usage), Partridge on slang, and the pamphlets of the Society for Pure English. Attwater's Dictionary of Saints was there, and its temporal counterpart, the Complete Peerage, which had a pedestal of its own, was also within arm's reach. On the top of this mobile compendium, selected new books sometimes lay. This was at times a bad eminence, designed for the exposure in a double sense, of authors deserving only of scorn and chastisement. A careless visitor, on seeing them, might reveal in himself, at the first touch, an inadequacy beyond pardon. With rising excitement, therefore, I noted one day upon this dangerous shelf a copy of Miss Sitwell's Green Song. As always, the least movement of one's eye was pounced upon; and with that sudden forward lunge of interest and enthusiasm which he had somehow preserved intact from Harvard and Balliol days, my host said "That's a very remarkable book. I had no idea there was poetry of that kind in the world any more. She's a real poet. When I first read those lines—how did they go?—

> *I who was once a golden woman like those who walk*
> *In the dark heavens—but am now grown old*
> *And sit by the fire, and see the fire grow cold*

I said to myself 'There's the old voice of poetry, the old incantatory magic come back again' ". He paused for one of those coughs which marked, as it were, the bar-lines of his conversation. " 'Yes' I said to myself 'Why, yes—if that doesn't beat the bugs!' ".

This homely image seemed to me not at all odd, for Mr. Pearsall Smith was a great enthusiast for simple, bodily tropes, and it occurred to me also that it was very probably with this same phrase that, sixty years earlier, he had punctuated a first reading of Leaves of Grass. As he went on to elaborate the honours, both public and private, which in a just world would be heaped upon the author of such work, I wondered in what terms I could make my own reverences to these poems. For some time I had known, along with many other readers of her work, that this poetry, always admirable and indeed spellbinding for its verbal audacity and mastery of historical technique, had suddenly acquired for itself a new dimension and become, in fact, the size of its time. The effect of a poem such as "Invocation" was that of an *aria parlante;* the recurrence of her favourite great open vowels, the exceptional span of phrase and almost stellar movement of cadence—all these recall Gluck, and are perfectly suited to the new extremes of feeling which she has begun to explore. Mechanical excellence is of course a first condition of great poetry; and here it becomes a source of limitless power. Those facets of Miss Sitwell's being which formerly conspired to present her as not one person, but many, had at last grown together—had become, in fact, a new strain in English poetry.

Others however are better fitted than I to comment upon these late poems, with their Atlantean burden. Turning to the earlier pieces, I enjoy distinguishing in them the strains which, now harmoniously combined, seemed once to involve a whole family of voices. There are lines which become a permanent part of landscape, as when

> *In the floating and mysterious leaves*
> *A silver sound like some forgotten music grieves*

Sometimes one surprises a novelist at work, condensing a whole character into a single phrase; a governess becomes, for instance, "a tiny spider in a gilded nut." Sometimes the objects of the visible world draw out a fantasist of Firbankian stature:

> *Castellated,*
> *Related*
> *To castles the waves lean*
> *Balmoral-like*

And at other times Miss Sitwell makes us free of the enchanted region conjured by the Chorus in "The Madness of Saul"—"the singing gardens of the Pleiades." These gardens, lost in the secretive countryside of England, glance out when they are least expected—when, for instance, Lily O'Grady

> *Walked by the cupolas, gables in the*
> *Lake's Georgian stables*

or when we seem suddenly to be lying

> *like Ophelia drowned in blond*
> *And fluid hair, beneath stag-antlered trees*

This sympathy, or rather identity with landscape has led recently to moments of such surpassing grandeur, visions in which the frontiers of our understanding are pushed on and outwards, that it is touching to recall earlier passages, such as those in which the Man from a Far Countree speaks of his longing to become

> *The peacefulness of a lovely tree*
> *A tree wherein the golden birds*
> *Are singing in the darkest branches, oh!*

106

Beside these first intimations of great themes, there are virtuoso-passages in which grotesque lines by Georgina Farrar acquire new dignity from their surroundings; by turns *conteur* and zoologist, Miss Sitwell reminds us of the foibles of Sir Rotherham Redde, Black Mrs. Behemoth and Captain Fracasse, "stout as any water-butt," until it is the turn of the giraffe or the honey-bee, and we learn that

> *The kangaroo, chaste,*
> *Of Victorian complexion,*
> *Wears at her waist*
> *Each pledge of affection.*

The black fountains of grief and despair have since played over many of these early themes. The nursery lullaby

> *Do, do,*
> *Princess, do*
> *The fairy Chatte Blanche rocks you slow*

rocks now to a terrible conclusion; and where once "an old woman lamented in springtime" in the strait four-footed line of a child's poetry notebook, there is now the great over-running statement of the late poems, in which a dozen long lines suffice barely for a single draught of this deep-breathing music. For the dilation of such a heart, no human image seems adequate, and one must go rather to the great creatures of the earth—the whale perhaps, whose heart is said to pump some ten or fifteen gallons at a time.

Such thoughts as these passed through my head, with the indiscipline of Bulgarian grenadiers, while Mr. Pearsall Smith was consulting with another guest as to whether the rites of the Anglican Church could not be amended to allow of Miss Sitwell's enthronement in Westminster Abbey. Suddenly he turned to me, his campaigner's eye aflame: "What about you?", he said, "Don't you think they are wonderful poems?"

The lapidary phrase fell from heaven. I felt my head thrust itself purposefully forward, and my jaw open to allow for the transmission of a final judgment.

"Yes, rather", I said, "I've always thought them jolly good stuff".

107

TRENDS IN THE POETRY OF EDITH SITWELL

L. P. Hartley

Nearly every important artist is to some extent an interpreter of his times, he gives the bent and impress of his mind to material that is already there; and this is true of Miss Edith Sitwell. She was in the van of the aesthetic renaissance that started in the first World War. That renaissance was also a reaction: a reaction against "mud and blood" and against the type of literature—realism or satire—that had been wallowing in mud and blood. The reaction took various forms. The 'Georgian' school of poets turned to nature, landscape and the country—they found, in meticulous observation of birds, trees, flowers and clouds, peace and healing for emotions excoriated by the war. The poetry of John Clare had a noteworthy revival, and

The lesser missel-thrush that perches
On the lower boughs of birches

suddenly enjoyed a tremendous vogue.

For Miss Sitwell, reaction from the war meant recoil from stereotyped emotions expressed in tired language, from the tyranny of the mind over the senses, from dull tones and safety-first tactics. She brought to poetry bright colours, hard shining surfaces, and a general electrification of moribund and sleepy words. The Ballet was then at its height. Miss Sitwell's poems danced a ballet and accepted the ballet's convention, its appeal to the mind through the senses, and its stylised emotion. Possibly this con-

108

vention owed something to French examples, but as it appeared, fully developed, in English literature, it was the invention of Miss Sitwell and her brothers, for in spite of differences in what they saw, they saw through the same eyes. In prose, a comparable achievement was Ronald Firbank's. He had the same gift for creating beauty, wit, humour and even pathos by applying a highly stylised point of view to the natural, the humdrum, and the familiar. Seen in the light of his sophistication the great out-of-doors became almost blushingly self-conscious.

Miss Sitwell, though she did not follow the example of the Georgian poets in their way of presenting Nature, was just as much inspired by Nature as they were. "I was brought up in the country," she writes in the preface to her Selected Poems, "and mine is a country world. The artificiality of which my poems are accused is such that when I write of emotion I try to strip the passion down to the barest possible expression, a quintessential simplicity. When my poems deal with emotion they are always the most simple and primitive emotions of simple and primitive people . . . I was born by the wildest seas that England knows, and my earliest recollection is of the tides, the wild rush of waves, the sweep onward, heard night and day, so that it seemed the sound of one's own blood.

That was in 1936. To those who are familiar with Miss Sitwell's poems written during the present war it may well seem grotesque that she was ever accused of artificiality. And, in any case, why "accused"? Why must "artificial" bear a pejorative meaning? The artificial is only to be avoided if it is a substitute for the real, and not always then. If it is used, as Miss Sitwell used it from the first, as her brothers used it and as Ronald Firbank used it, to heighten the reality of an object or an idea, to surprise it into a new vividness of meaning—then there can be no objection to artificiality. As well object to a lantern on the ground that its light is artificial. What we want is to see, and any device that helps towards that is laudable, however artificial it may be.

Perhaps to revive the question of Miss Sitwell's 'artificiality' at this time of day is to flog a dead horse. But even if her early work is artificial, I still think that a new way of looking at things, tending to reveal reality rather than to obscure it, is a merit, not a defect.

A new way of looking at things was one of Miss Sitwell's contributions to the poetry of our day. "My senses," she says, "are interchangeable; where the language of one sense is insufficient to convey a meaning, a sensation, I use another." All poets have done this, more or less; the difference is that whereas their borrowings are often involuntary, Miss Sitwell's are nearly always deliberate, an intentional transference of the language of one sense to another. Often they need no explanation: "furred is the light" refers to misty moonlight; the "reynard-coloured sun" explains itself, as do the "cotton-nightcap trees". And if some of the allusions are, as Miss Sitwell herself says, to recondite, e.g., "the Martha-coloured scabious" and the "Emily-coloured primulas", still they are enriching, even if we are not aware that Miss Sitwell's nursery maid, Martha, once wore a scabious-coloured gown and that the primula reminded the poet of the bright pink cheeks of country girls, so often christened Emily. Moreover, her linking together of a flower, a colour, and a human being, as though all three were aspects of the same thing, is very characteristic of her philosophy, which is unifying, and intent on discovering the essential likeness in all created things. I shall return to this, for it is a vital principle of her poetry.

Though one of the most individual, Miss Sitwell is one of the least personal of poets, if by personal one means a poet who writes for the sake of self-expression. The word 'I' seldom occurs in her poetry and if it does, there is no weight of egoism behind it. She is the vehicle, not the subject, of her inspiration. Again, she tells us that many of her early poems—those in *Facade*, for instance, "are, for the most part, abstract patterns, difficult technical experiments . . . inquiries into the effect on rhythm and on speed, of the use of rhymes, assonances and dissonances, placed outwardly, at different places in the line, in most elaborate patterns. . . ."

It is unwise to quarrel with an author's definition of his own work, and if Miss Sitwell says the poems in *Facade* are abstract

110

patterns and technical experiments, then they are. But I submit
that they are a good deal besides. At the word "experiment" in
connexion with literature (and indeed in connexion with science)
one's heart sinks; one remembers the brilliant talents—Gertrude
Stein's, James Joyce's—that have gone astray in the mazes of word-
patterns, forsaking meaning to achieve—what? Certain aesthetic
effects perceptible to an ear attuned, but even at their most successful constituting an esoteric game to be enjoyed by the few
and even by them only with the help, (one suspects), of a good
deal of self-deception. And the sound-effects Miss Sitwell analyses
so minutely are not, it should be noted, effects that belong exclu-
sively or even mainly to an abstract pattern; her choice and placing
of vowels and consonants may be, and no doubt are, deliberate,
but as she abundantly shows, they are intended to make clear the
meaning of the poem, to hasten its message to the mind, whereas
a pattern has only value to the eye. In her *Poets' Note Book* Miss
Sitwell observes that "the poet's mind has become a central
sense, interpreting and controlling this and the five senses." If
the mind (pace Helvetius) is "the product of the senses" it cannot be satisfied with the evidence of one of them.

Most readers get from *Facade* images more precise and meanings more articulate than any that could be conveyed by a word-
pattern and it is inevitable they should, for as Miss Sitwell herself
says of these poems, "Some deal with materialism and the world
crumbling into dust, some have as protagonists shadows or ghosts,
moving, not in my country world, but in a highly mechanical
universe; others have beings moving:

> To the small sound of Time's drum in the heart,
> figures gesticulating against the darkness, from the warmth
> and light of their little candle-show

Just so; the poems have a subject, they are about something.
In literature a word-pattern must be a means to a meaning, it
cannot stand by itself, as it does in a carpet. So that in these
poems we have meaning as well as music, sense as well as sound.

Facade was written in 1922, a year when the ordinary ob-
server did not suspect that the world was crumbling to dust, far

from it. Most poets are prophets, and Miss Sitwell can claim the gift of prophecy in a special degree.

In this connexion one is reminded that though she has written at some length about the technique of her poetry, she has said very little about the ideas underlying it, and about her personal experience as a poet, almost nothing.

We must admire her reticence, the reticence of a craftsman to whom his craft is more important than his own performance in it. Miss Sitwell's enthusiasm is for poetry, not for herself as a poet. Her verses do not unlock her heart. Her attitude towards her poetry has always been strictly professional; hers is

> *The strain seraphically free*
> *From taint of personality.*

But poetry springs from emotion, whether recollected in tranquillity or pouring into the ink that flows from the poet's pen. Anyone reading "Gold Coast Customs" for the first time must be overwhelmed by the emotion it arouses. It acts on the nerves of the mind like a violent irritant; and we ask, from what reservoir of feeling does this spiritual vitriol come? Miss Sitwell herself answers the question in a most illuminating note—one of the few that answers the 'why' of her poetry instead of the 'how'.

"The organisation of the poem, of a world where all the natural rhythms of the spirit, of the soil, and of the seasons have broken down, but where a feverish intertwining seething movement, a vain seeking for excitement, still exists, presented considerable difficulties." She goes on to speak of "this world of the rich man Judas, brother Cain," where "man is part ravenous beast of prey, part worm, part ogre, or is but the worm turned vertebrate. It is a world where the light is no longer a reality, but a high ventriloquist sound (so high none knows whence it comes), the octave of the black clotted night—no longer the true and guiltless Light:

> (*"Christ that takest away the sin*
> *Of the world, and the rich man's bone-dead grin"*)

112

This is all I can bring myself to say about the poem except from a technical point of view."

Later she writes:

"Throughout the whole poem I have tried to produce, not so much the record of a world, as the wounded and suffering soul of that world, its living evocation, not its history, and seen through the eyes of a protagonist whose personal tragedy is echoed in that vaster tragedy. Of the other implicit meanings of the poem I am unwilling to speak."

No one could have written "Gold Coast Customs" without suffering. Indeed, the poem is suffering, suffering in the raw, suffering that is felt along the nerves like a tooth being pulled out, suffering that the mind has not had time to assimilate. It is almost the only poem of Miss Sitwell's that is aimed primarily at the reader's nerves. It is not her best poem, but it is terribly effective and it marks a turning-point in her poetic development. It is a kind of watershed dividing the stream of her work into two valleys, one of which, the narrower, is all sunshine, and the other, broad and still broadening out, is the valley with which her war poems have made us familiar, a tremendous landscape embracing many climates, many temperatures from torrid heat to polar cold, in which the features are enormous but less sharply defined, and in which the antitheses are on the grandest possible scale, day and night, summer and winter, life and death.

In the one there is no explicit and comparatively little underlying philosophy. Things perceived through the senses wear their face value, their value to the senses; beauty, in such poems as "The Soldan's Song" and "Most Lovely Shade", is an invocation from words and sounds and images, almost unrelated to human emotion, saved from abstraction only by the vague pathos, the sense of too much beauty, creating a need it cannot quite satisfy, that we feel in the pictures of Giorgione (Miss Sitwell's romantic mood has much in common with his). These poems are sufficient in themselves; they raise no questions and expect no answers, any more than do those gossamer, decorative pieces, "Through Gilded Trellises" and "The Governante's Song," and "Lily O' Grady," that take the ear with the delicate rattle of castanets. We are in a pagoda country, superimposed on an English landscape, guests as it were of an Eastern potentate or a magician whose whim it is to charm and divert us; strange words—pelongs, buchauls, pallampores—woo us with soft sounds; braying words—brocade, promenade, arcade, ambassade, startle us with harsh ones; ingenious rhymes tickle our ears, the lines are short and staccato, and the pace break-neck. And if a hint of suffering creeps in, as it sometimes does:

> Jane, Jane
> Forget the pain
> In your heart. Go, work again!

it is quickly and discreetly banished. And the mythological personages who haunt these scenes are queens and princesses, rustics and milk-maids, or "Chinoiserie ghosts" whose emotions need never be taken seriously.

Of course the division is not water-tight; some of these earlier poems (the "Four Elegies", for instance), are as sad, if not quite the same depth of suffering, as any Miss Sitwell has written. But in the main it holds good. If her high spirits were not so spontaneous (few poets have written poems as cloudless and carefree as some of these) one might be tempted to think them poems of escape, happy images that Miss Sitwell has summoned to keep the others out, forced smiles to hold tears at bay.

For as all students know, the latter poems, heralded by "Still Falls the Rain," and "Lullaby" and "Serenade" and "Street Song", are so different in form and feeling and intention that they might almost be the work of another mind. The lines are long—as long as the rollers that break on that northern shore where Miss Sitwell lived as a child; they are often, though not always, unrhymed; their pulse beats strong but slow, there is a note of longing in them, and the ache of suffering is never absent. They do not, as did "Gold Coast Customs," play upon the nerves; their appeal is to the mind and the heart. They are utterly serious, not only as works of art—Miss Sitwell has always been a serious artist—but as criticisms of life. They stand up to the most terrible phenomena of the present day, the atom bomb and con-

114

centration camp; they are indeed the only poems of our time that accept the challenge of the War, that look, not unmoved, but undismayed, on "the flag of blood flying across the world," that recognise, without despairing, "the ultimate cold within the heart of man."

At least, I think Miss Sitwell does not despair. Like other poets she has moods, and it would be idle to pretend that she is not sometimes a pessimist. *The Song of the Cold*, that gives its title to her latest book, is an utterance heavy with doom:

> "Have you too known the cold?
> Give me your hand to warm me. I am no more alone.
> There was a sun that shone
> On all alike, but the cold in the heart of Man
> Has slain it. Where is it gone?"

In "The Two Loves" she writes:

> We might tell the blind
> The hue of the flower, or the philosopher
> What distance is, in the essence of its being—
> But not the distance between the hearts of Men.

We may guess what it must have cost Miss Sitwell emotionally to turn—to be compelled to turn—away from the bright scene of her poetry's childhood to these lightless limbos of her later imagining—

> Where fallen man and the rising ape
> And the howling Dark play games,

especially when she remembers that

> ... There was a planet dancing in my mind
> with a gold seed of Folly ... long ago ...

The poems get much of their power from the fact that she has written them, one suspects, à contre-coeur; she does not taste a luxury in grief, she finds no release in moral indignation; we feel her whole nature protesting against the company it keeps, the Worm, the Ape, the Skeleton, the crouching tiger and

> Man's threatening shadow
> Red-edged by the sun like Cain,

—and pining, like Proserpine or Eurydice, for the fields of spring, in which, until quite lately, she sometimes took a holiday, as witness the ecstatic "How Many Heavens" which soars like a lark's song above the terrifying charnel noises of "Street Songs". Goethe said that you must ask birds and children if you want to know how strawberries taste. "In these respects, I for one am both child and bird," is Miss Sitwell's comment. To write these poems she has had to put away childish things, and to renounce the birdsong; yet again and again she returns to the positive, life-giving symbols of the Sun, the Lion, and the Rose; opposing the elements in man that make for happiness and survival to those that are suicidal and destructive. She believes in the kinship of all created things, one might almost say, she believes they are identical; and this belief enables her, as she suggests in her poem, "An Old Woman", to accept sorrow and even death without complaining, even with a kind of rejoicing, when they conform to nature's pattern, to the seasons' cycle of birth, maturity and decay:

> Though the dust, the shining racer, overtake me,
> I too was a golden woman like those that walk
> In the fields of the heavens . . .

It is (I think) the suspicion that man has somehow cast himself adrift from the order of Nature, and become like a cancer in the body of creation, a roving cell blindly bent on mischief, that disturbs her; the fear that human beings may have put themselves outside the pale of human compassion. From this dread she seeks refuge by contemplating the sufferings of Christ:

> Still falls the rain—
> Still falls the Blood from the Starved Man's wounded Side:
> He bears in His Heart all wounds . . .

This is one of the few instances in which Miss Sitwell makes open avowal of the Christian faith. Christianity may be implicit in all her thoughts; it shows again and again in her imagery, in her preoccupation with the parable of Dives and Lazarus, in her forbearance and in her compassion. But suffering, as I tried to point out, is alien to her; she does not accept it as many Christians

116

would do, as an inevitable consequence of the Fall. These great poems are written in anguish but the bent of her mind is towards rejoicing, as was Blake's and Whitman's and Smart's; "the emeralds are singing on the grasses," and she would fain sing with them. She is not a long-faced poet. In a world without Gold Coast Customs, without total wars, she could find in the mere appearances of things the same spiritual delight that visited Thomas Traherne when he looked on the orient and immortal wheat. But now, when

> The pulse that beats in the heart is changed to the hammer
> That sounds in the Potter's Field

she feels, perhaps, that the spirit has lost its bearings, and that humanity no longer has the power to heal its own wounds. And it is significant that in the last poem in her latest book, after recalling the names of poets and scientists who have felt in themselves the Divine Principle or sought it in creation, she invokes:

> ... One who contracted His Immensity
> And shut Himself in the scope of a small flower ...

and cries, "with the voice of Fire"

> Will he disdain that flower of the world, the heart of Man?

117

GOLD COAST CUSTOMS

One fantee wave
Is grave and tall
As brave Ashantee's
Thick mud wall.
Munza rattles his bones in the dust,
Lurking in murk because he must.

Striped black and white
Is the squealing light;
The dust brays white in the market place,
Dead powder spread on a black skull's face.

Like monkey-skin
Is the sea — one sin
Like a weasel is nailed to bleach on the rocks
Where the eyeless mud screeched fawning, mocks

At a negro that wipes
His knife . . . dug there,
A bugbear bellowing
Bone dared rear —
A bugbear bone that bellows white
As the ventriloquist sound of light,

It rears at his head-dress of felted black hair
The one humanity clinging there —
His eyeless face whitened like black and white bones
And his beard of rusty
Brown grass cones

Hard blue and white
Cowrie shells (the light
Grown hard) outline
The leopard-skin musty
Leaves that shine
With an animal smell both thick and fusty.

One house like a rat-skin
Mask flaps fleet ·
In the sailor's tall
Ventriloquist street
Where the rag houses flap —
Hiding a gap.

Here, tier on tier
Like a black box rear
₁In the flapping slum
Beside Death's docks.
I did not know this meaner Death
Meant this: that the bunches of nerves still dance
And caper among these slums, and prance.

'Mariners, put your bones to bed!'
But at Lady Bamburghers' parties each head,
Grinning, knew it left its bones
In the mud with the white skulls . . . only the grin
Is left, strings of nerves, and the drum-taut skin.

When the sun in the empty
Sky is high
In his dirty brown and white
Bird-skin dress —
He hangs like a skull
With a yellow dull
Face made of clay
(Where tainted, painted the plague-spots bray)
To hide where the real face rotted away.
So our worm-skin and paper masks still keep,
Above the rotting bones they hide,
The marks of the Plague whereof we died:
The belief,
The grief,
The love,
Or the grin
Of the shapeless worm-soft unshaping Sin —

120

Unshaping till no more the beat of the blood
Can raise up the body from the endless mud
Though the hell-fires cold
As the worm, and old,
Are painted upon each unshaped form —
No more man, woman, or beast to see —
But the universal devouring Worm.

When the sun of dawn looks down on the shrunken
Heads, drums of skin, and the dead men drunken,
I only know one half of my heart
Lies in that terrible coffin of stone,
My body that stalks through the slum alone.
And that half of my heart
That is in your breast
You gave for meat
In the sailors street
To the rat that had only my bones to eat.

But those hardened hearts
That roll and sprawl,
In a cowl of foul blind monkey-skin,
Lest the whips of the light crash roaring in —
Those hearts that roll
Down the phantom street
They have for their beat
The cannibal drums
And the cries of the slums,
And the Bamburgher parties — they have them all!
One high house flaps . . . taps
Light's skin drum —

Monkey-like shrunk
On all fours now come
The parties' sick ghosts, each hunting himself —
Black gaps beneath an apes thick pelt,

Chasing a rat,
Their souls ghost fat
Through the negro swamp,
Slum hovel's cramp,
Of Lady Bamburgher's parties above
With the latest grin, and the latest love,
And the latest game:
To show the shame
Of the rat-fat soul to the grinning day
With even the rat-skin flayed away.

Now, a thick cloud floating
Low o'er the lake,
Millions of flies
Begin to awake,
With the animation
Of smart conversation:
From Bedlam's madness the thick gadflies
Seek for the broken statue's eyes.

Where the mud and the murk
Whispering lurk:
'From me arises everything,
The negro's louse,
The armadillo,
Munza's bone and his peccadillo.'

Where flaps degraded
The black and sated
Slack macerated
And antiquated
Beckoning negress
Nun of the shade,
And the rickety houses

Rock and rot,
Lady Bamburgher airs

That foul plague-spot
Her romantic heart.
From the cannibal mart,
That smart Plague-cart,
Lady Bamburgher rolls where the foul newsheet
And the shambles for souls are set in the street.

And stuck in front
Of this world-tall Worm,
Stuck in front
Of this world's confession —
Like something rolled
Before a procession,
Is the face, a flimsy worm-skin thing
That someone has raked
From the low plague-pit
As a figure-head
For Corruption dead,
And a mask for the universal Worm.

Her ape-skin yellow
Tails of hair
Clung about her bone-white bare
Eyeless mask that cackled there:

The Worm's mask hid
Her eyeless mud,
Her shapeless love,
The plot to escape
From the God-ordained shape

And her soul, the cannibal
Amazon's mart,
Where in squealing light
And clotted black night
On the monkey-skin black and white striped dust they
Cackle and bray to the murdered day.

And the Amazon queen
With a bone-black face
Wears a mask with an ape-skin beard; she grinds
Her male child's bones in a mortar, binds
Him for food, and the people buy.   For this

Hidden behind
The Worm's mask grown
White as a bone
Where eyeholes rot wide
And are painted for sight,
And the little mouth red as a dead Plague-spot
On that white mask painted to hide Death's rot,

For this painted Plague-cart's
Heart, for this
Slime of the Worm that paints her kiss
And the dead men's bones round her throat and wrist,
The half of my heart that lay in your breast
Has fallen away
To rot and bray
With the painted mud through the eyeless day.

The dust of all the dead can blow
Backwards and forwards, to and fro
To cover the half of my heart with death's rot,
Yet the dust of that other half comes not
To this coffin of stone that stalks through the slum,
Though love to you now is the deaf Worm's lust
That, cloven in halves, will re-unite
Foulness to deadness in the dust
And chaos of the enormous night.

How far is our innocent paradise,
The blue-striped sand,
Bull-bellowing band
Of waves, and the great gold suns made wise
By the dead days and the horizons grand.

124

Can a planet tease
With its great gold train,
Walking beside the pompous main —
That great gold planet the heat of the Sun
Where we saw black Shadow, a black man, run,
So a negress dare
Wear long gold hair?
The negress Dorothy one sees
Beside the caverns and the trees
Where her parasol
Throws a shadow tall
As a waterfall —
The negress Dorothy still feels
The great gold planet tease her brain.

And dreaming deep within her blood
Lay Africa like the dark in the wood;
For Africa is the unhistorical,
Unremembering, unrhetorical,
Undeveloped spirit involved
In the conditions of nature — Man,
That black image of stone hath delved
On the threshold where history began.

Now under the cannibal
Sun is spread
The black rhinoceros-hide of the mud
For endlessness and timelessness . . . dead
Grass creaks like a carrion-bird's voice, rattles,
Squeaks like a wooden shuttle.   Battles
Have worn this deserted skeleton black
As empty chain armour . . . lazily back

With only the half of its heart it lies
With the giggling mud devouring its eyes,
Naught left to fight
But the black clotted night
In its heart, and ventriloquist squealing light.

But lying beneath the giggling mud
I thought there was something living, the bray
Of the eyeless mud can not betray —
Though it is buried beneath black bones
Of the fetiches screeching like overtones
Of the light, as they feel the slaves' spilt blood.

In tiers like a box
Beside the docks
The negro prays,
The negro knocks.
'Is Anyone there?'
His mumblings tear
Nothing but paper walls, and the blare
Of the gaping capering empty air.
The cannibal drums still roll in the mud
To the bones of the king's mother laved in blood
And the trophies with long black hair, shrunken heads
That drunken, shrunk upon tumbled beds.

The negro rolls
His red eyeballs
Prostrates himself.
The negro sprawls:
His God is but a flat black stone
Upright upon a squeaking bone.

The negro's dull
Red eyeballs roll . . .
The immortality of the soul
Is but black ghosts that squeak through the hole
That once seemed eyes in Munza's skull.

This is his god:
The cannibal sun
On bones that played
For evermore,

And the dusty roar
Of the ancient Dead,
And the squealing rat,
The soul's ghost fat.
But Lady Bamburgher's Shrunken Head,

Slum hovel, is full of the rat-eaten bones
Of a fashionable god that lived not
Ever, but still has bones to rot:
A bloodless and an unborn thing
That cannot wake, yet cannot sleep,
That makes no sound, that cannot weep,
That hears all, bears all, cannot move —
It is buried so deep
Like a shameful thing
In that plague-spot heart, Death's last dust-heap.

A tall house flaps
In the canvas street,
Down in the wineshop
The Amazons meet
With the tall abbess
Of the shade. . . .
A ghost in a gown
Like a stiff brigade

Watches the sailor
With a guitar
Lure the wind
From the islands far.

O far horizons and bright blue wine
And majesty of the seas that shine,
Bull-bellowing waves that ever fall
Round the god-like feet and the goddess tall!

A great yellow flower
With the silence shy

To the wind from the islands
Sighs 'I die.'

At the foot of the steps
Like the navy-blue ghost
Of a coiling negro,
In dock slums lost,
(The ghost haunting steamers
And cocktail bars,
Card-sharpers, schemers,
And Pullman cars)

A ripple rose
With mud at its root
And weeping kissed
A statue's foot.

In the sailor's tall
Ventriloquist street
The calico dummies
Flap and meet:
Calculate: 'Sally go
Pick up a sailor.'
Behind that facade
The worm is a jailer.

'I cannot stiffen . . . I left my bones
Down in the street: no overtones
Of the murdered light can join my dust
To my black bones pressed in the House of Lust.
Only my feet still walk in the street;
But where is my heart and its empty beat?

"Starved silly Sally, why dilly and dally?"
The dummies said when I was a girl.
The rat deserts a room that is bare,
But Want, a cruel rat gnawing there
Ate to the heart, all else was gone,

Nothing remained but Want alone.
So now I'm a gay girl, a calico dummy,
With nothing left alive but my feet
That walk up and down in the Sailor's Street.

Behind the bawdy hovels like hoardings
Where harridans peer from the grovelling boarding
House, the lunatic
Wind still shakes
My empty rag-body, nothing wakes;
The wind like a lunatic in a fouled
Nightgown, whipped those rags and howled.

Once I saw it come
Through the canvas slum,
Rattle and beat what seemed a drum,
Rattle and beat it with a bone.
O Christ, that bone was dead, alone.
Christ, who will speak to such ragged Dead
As me, I am dead, alone and bare,
They expose me still to the grinning air;
I shall never gather my bones and my dust
Together (so changed and scattered, lost . . .)
So I can be decently buried!
What is that whimpering like a child
That this mad ghost beats like a drum in the air?
The heart of Sal
That once was a girl
And now is a calico thing to loll
Over the easy steps of the slum
Waiting for something dead to come.'

From Rotten Alley and Booble Street,
The beggars crawl to starve near the meat
Of the reeling appalling cannibal mart,
And Lady Bamgurgher, smart Plague-cart.
Red rag face and a cough that tears
They creep through the mud of the docks from their lairs;

129

And when the dog-whining dawn light
Nosed for their hearts, whined in fright,
With a sly high animal
Whimpering, half-frightened call
To worlds outside our consciousness
It finds no heart within their dress.
The Rat has eaten
That and beaten
Hope and love and memory,
At last, and even the will to die.
But what is the loss?   For you cannot sell
The heart to those that have none for Hell
To fatten on . . . or that cheap machine,
And its beat would make springs for the dancing feet
Of Lady Bamburgher down in the street
Of her dogs that nose out each other's sin,
And grin, and whine, and roll therein.

Against the Sea-wall are painted signs
'Here for a shilling a sailor dines.'
Each Rag-and-Bone
Is propped up tall
(Lest in death it fall)
Against the Sea-wall.
Their empty mouths are sewed up whole
Lest from hunger they gape and cough up their soul.
The arms of one are stretched out wide. . . .
How long, since our Christ was crucified?

Rich man Judas,
Brother Cain,
The rich men are your worms that gain
The air through seething from your brain;
Judas, mouldering in your old
Coffin body, still undying
As the Worm, where you are lying
With no flesh for warmth, but gold
For flesh, for warmth, for sheet,

Now you are fleshless, too, as these
That starve and freeze,
Is your gold hard as Hell's huge polar street,
Is the universal blackness of Hell's day so cold?

When, creeping over
The Sailor's Street
Where the houses like rat-skin
Masks flap, meet
Never across the murdered bone
Of the sailor, the whining overtone
Of dawn sounds, slaves
Rise from their graves,
Where in the corpse-sheet night they lay
Forgetting the mutilating day,
Like the unborn child in its innocent sleep.
Ah Christ, the murdered light must weep —
(Christ that takest away the sin
Of the world, and the rich man's bone-dead grin)
The light must weep
Seeing that sleep
And those slaves rise up in their death-chains, part
The light from the eyes
The hands from the heart,
Since their hearts are flesh for the tall
And sprawling
Reeling appalling
Cannibal mart,
But their hands and head
Are machines to breed
Gold for the old and the greedy Dead.

I have seen the murdered God look through the eyes
Of the drunkard's smirched
Mask as he lurched
O'er the half of my heart that lies in the street
Neath the dancing fleas and the foul news-sheet.

Where (a black gap flapping,
A white skin drum)
The cannibal houses
Watch this come —
Lady Bamburgher's party; for the plan
Is a prize for those that on all fours ran
Through the rotting slum
Till those who come
Could never guess from the mud-covered shapes
Which are the rich or the mired dire apes,
As they run where the souls, dirty paper, are blown
In the hour before dawn, through this long hell of stone.

Perhaps if I too lie down in the mud,
Beneath tumbrils rolling
And mad skulls galloping
Far from their bunches of nerves that dance
And caper among these slums and prance,
Beneath the noise of that hell that rolls
I shall forget the shrunken souls
The eyeless mud squealing 'God is dead,'
Starved men (bags of wind) and the harlot's tread,
The heaven turned into monkey-hide
By Lady Bamburgher's dancing fleas,
Her rotting parties and death-slack ease,
And the dead men drunken
(The only tide)
Blown up and down
And tossed through the town
Over the half of my heart that lies
Deep down, in this meaner Death, with cries.
The leaves of black hippopotamus-hide
Black as the mud
Cover the blood
And the rotting world. Do we smell and see

The sick thick smoke from London burning,
Gomorrah turning

Like worms in the grave,
The Bedlam daylight's murderous roar,
Those pillars of fire the drunkard and whore,
Dirty souls boiled in cannibal cookshops to paper
To make into newspapers, flags? . . . They caper
Like gaping apes.   Foul fires we see,
For Bedlam awakes to reality.

The drunkard burning,
The skin drums galloping,
In their long march still parched for the sky,
The Rotten Alleys where beggars groan
And the beggar and his dog share a bone;
The rich man Cain that hides within
His lumbering palaces where Sin
Through the eyeless holes of Day peers in,
The murdered heart that all night turns
From small machine to shapeless Worm
With hate, and like Gomorrah burns —
These put the eyes of Heaven out,
These raise all Hell's throats to a shout,
These break my heart's walls toppling in,
And like a universal sea
The nations of the Dead crowd in.

Bahunda, Banbangala, Barumbe, Bonge,
And London fall, . . . rolling human skin drums
Surrounded by long black hair, I hear
Their stones that fall,
Their voices that call,
Among the black and the bellowing bones.
But yet when the cannibal
Sun is high
The sightless mud
Weeps tears, a sigh,
To rhinoceros-hided leaves: 'Ah why
So sightless, earless, voiceless, I?'

The mud has at least its skulls to roll;
But here as I walk, no voices call,
Only the stones and the bones that fall;
But yet if only one soul would whine,
Rat-like from the lowest mud, I should know
That somewhere in God's vast love it would shine;
But even the rat-whine has guttered low.

I saw the Blind like a winding-sheet
Tossed up and down through the blind man's street
Where the dead plague-spot
Of the spirit's rot
On the swollen thick houses
Cries to the quick,
Cries to the dark soul that lies there and dies
In hunger and murk, and answers not.

Gomorrah's fires have washed my blood —
But the fires of God shall wash the mud
Till the skin drums rolling
The slum cries sprawling
And crawling
Are calling
'Burn thou me!'
Though Death has taken
And pig-like shaken
Rooted and tossed
The rags of me.
Yet the time will come
To the heart's dark slum
When the rich man's gold and the rich man's wheat
Will grow in the street, that the starved may eat, —
And the sea of the rich will give up its dead —
And the last blood and fire from my side will be shed.
For the fires of God go marching on.

STILL FALLS THE RAIN

Still falls the Rain —
Dark as the world of man, black as our loss —
Blind as the nineteen hundred and forty nails
Upon the Cross.

Still falls the Rain
With a sound like the pulse of the heart that is changed to the
  hammer-beat
In the Potter's Field, and the sound of the impious feet

On the Tomb
    Still falls the Rain
In the Field of Blood where the small hopes breed and the human
  brain
Nurtures its greed, that worm with the brow of Cain.

Still falls the Rain
At the feet of the Starved Man hung upon the Cross.
Christ that each day, each night, nails there, have mercy on us—
On Dives and on Lazarus:
Under the Rain the sore and the gold are as one.

Still falls the Rain
Still falls the Blood from the Starved Man's wounded Side:
He bears in His Heart all wounds,—those of the light that died,
The last faint spark
In the self-murdered heart, the wounds of the sad uncompre-
  hending dark,
The wounds of the baited bear,—
The blind and weeping bear whom the keepers beat
On his helpless flesh . . . the tears of the hunted hare.

Still falls the Rain —
Then—O Ile leape up to my God: who pulles me doune —
See, see where Christ's blood streames in the firmament:

135

It flows from the Brow we nailed upon the tree
Deep to the dying, to the thirsting heart
That holds the fires of the world,—dark-smirched with pain,
As Caesar's laurel crown.
Then sounds the voice of One who like the heart of man
Was once a child who among beasts has lain —
' Still do I love, still shed my innocent light, my Blood, for thee.'

LULLABY

Though the world has slipped and gone,
Sounds my loud discordant cry
Like the steel birds' song on high:
' Still one thing is left — the Bone! '
Then out danced the Babioun.

She sat in the hollow of the sea —
A socket whence the eye's put out —
She sang to the child a lullaby
(The steel birds' nest was thereabout).

' Do, do, do, do —
Thy mother's hied to the vaster race:
The Pterodactyl made its nest
And laid a steel egg in her breast —
Under the Judas-coloured sun.
She'll work no more, nor dance, nor moan
And I am come to take her place
Do, do.

There's nothing left but earth's low bed —
(The Pterodactyl fouls its nest):
But steel wings fan thee to thy rest,
And wingless truth and larvae lie

And eyeless hope and handless fear —
All these for thee as toys are spread,
Do — do —

Red is the bed of Poland, Spain,
And thy mother's breast, who has grown wise
In that fouled nest.   If she could rise,
Give birth again,

In wolfish pelt she'd hide thy bones
To shield thee from the world's long cold,
And down on all fours shouldst thou crawl
For thus from no height canst thou fall —
Do, do.

She'd give no hands: there's nought to hold
And nought to make: there's dust to sift,
But no food for the hands to lift.
Do, do.

Heed, my ragged lullaby,
Fear not living, fear not chance;
All is equal — blindness, sight,
There is no depth, there is no height:
Do, do.

The Judas-coloured sun is gone,
And with the Ape thou art alone —
Do,
    Do.'

SERENADE: ANY MAN TO ANY WOMAN

Dark angel who art clear and straight
As cannon shining in the air,
Your blackness doth invade my mind
And thunderous as the armoured wind
That rained on Europe is your hair;
And so I love you till I die —

(Unfaithful I, the cannon's mate) :
Forgive my love of such brief span,
But fickle is the flesh of man,
And death's cold puts the passion out.

I'll woo you with a serenade —
The wolfish howls the starving made;
And lies shall be your canopy
To shield you from the freezing sky.

Yet when I clasp you in my arms —
Who are my sleep, the zero hour
That clothes, instead of flesh, my heart, —
You in my heaven have no part,
For you, my mirage broken in flower,

Can never see what dead men know!
Then die with me and be my love:
The grave shall be your shady grove
And in your pleasaunce rivers flow

(To ripen this new Paradise)
From a more universal Flood
Than Noah knew: but yours is blood.

Yet still you will imperfect be
That in my heart like death's chill grows,
— A rainbow shining in the night,
Born of my tears . . . your lips, the bright
Summer-old folly of the rose.

STREET SONG

' Love my heart for an hour, but my bone for a day —
At least the skeleton smiles, for it has a morrow:
But the hearts of the young are now the dark treasure of Death,
And summer is lonely.

Comfort the lonely light and the sun in its sorrow,
Come like the night, for terrible is the sun
As truth, and the dying light shows only the skeleton's hunger
For peace, under the flesh like the summer rose.

Come through the darkness of death, as once through the
        branches
Of youth you came, through the shade like the flowering door
That leads into Paradise, far from the street,— you, the unborn
City seen by the homeless, the night of the poor.

You walk in the city ways, where Man's threatening shadow
Red-edged by the sun like Cain, has a changing shape —
Elegant like the Skeleton, crouched like the Tiger,
With the age-old wisdom and aptness of the Ape.

The pulse that beats in the heart is changed to the hammer
That sounds in the Potter's Field where they build a new world
From our Bone, and the carrion-bird days' foul droppings and
        clamour —
But you are my night, and my peace,

The holy night of conception, of rest, the consoling
Darkness when all men are equal, — the wrong and the right,
And the rich and the poor are no longer separate nations, —
They are brothers in night.'

This was the song I heard; but the Bone is silent!
Who knows if the sound was that of the dead light calling, —
Of Ceasar rolling onward his heart, that stone,
Or the burden of Atlas falling.

GREEN FLOWS THE RIVER OF LETHE—O

Green flows the river of Lethe—O
Long Lethe river
Where the fire was in the veins—and grass is growing
Over the fever —
The green grass growing . . .

I stood near the Cities of the Plains
And the young girls were chasing their hearts like the gay butterflies
Over the fields of summer —
O evanescent velvets fluttering your wings
Like winds and butterflies on the Road from Nothing to Nowhere!

But in the summer drought
I fled, for I was a Pillar of Fire, I was Destruction
Unquenched, incarnate and incarnadine.

I was Annihilation
Yet white as the Dead Sea, white as the Cities of the Plains.
For I listened to the noontide and my veins
That threatened thunder and the heart of roses.

I went the way I would —
But long is the terrible Street of the Blood
That had once seemed only part of the summer redness:
It stretches for ever, and there is no turning
But only fire, annihilation, burning.

I thought the way of the Blood would never tire
But now only the red clover
Lies over the breath of the lion and the mouth of the lover —

And green flows the Lethe river — O
Long Lethe river
Over Gomorrah's city and the fire. . . .

A MOTHER TO HER DEAD CHILD

The winter, the animal sleep of the earth is over
And in the warmth of the affirming sun
All beings, beasts, men, planets, waters, move
Freed from the imprisoning frost, acclaim their love
That is the light of the sun.

So the first spring began

Within the heart before the Fall of Man.

The earth puts forth its sprays, the heart its warmth
And your hands push back the dark that is your nurse,
Feel for my heart as in the days before your birth.
O Sun of my life, return to the waiting earth
Of your mother's breast, the heart, the empty arms.
Come soon, for the time is passing, and when I am old
The night of my body will be too thick and cold
For the sun of your growing heart.   Return from your new mother
The earth: she is too old for your little body,
Too old for the small tendernesses, the kissings
In the soft tendrils of your hair.   The earth is so old
She can only think of darkness and sleep, forgetting
That children are restless like the small spring shadows.
But the huge pangs of winter and the pain
Of the spring's birth, the endless centuries of rain
Will not lay bare your trusting smile, your tress,
Or lay your heart bare to my heart again
In your small earthly dress.
And when I wait for you upon the summer roads
They bear all things and men, business and pleasure, sorrow,
And lovers' meetings, mourning shades, the poor man's leisure,
And the foolish rose that cares not ever for the far tomorrow.
But the roads are too busy for the sound of your feet,
And the lost men, the rejected of life, who tend the wounds
That life has made as if they were a new sunrise, whose human
      speech is dying
From want, to the rusted voice of the tiger, turn not their heads lest

141

I hear your child-voice crying
In that hoarse tiger-voice: ' I am hungry! am cold!'
Lest I see your smile upon lips that were made for the kiss that
    exists not,
The food that deserts them,—those lips never warm with love, but
    from the world's fever,
Whose smile is a gap into darkness, the breaking apart,
Of the long-impending earthquake that waits in the heart.
That smile rends the soul with the sign of its destitution,
It drips from the last long pangs of the heart, self-devouring,
And tearing the seer.

                Yet one will return to the lost men,
Whose heart is the Sun of Reason, dispelling the shadow
That was born with no eyes to shed tears, — bringing peace to the
    lust
And pruriency of the Ape, from the human heart's sublimity
And tenderness teaching the dust that it is holy,
And to those who are hungry, are naked and cold as the worm,
    who are bare as the spirit
In that last night when the rich and the poor are alone,
Bringing love like the daily bread, like the light at morning.
And knowing this, I would give you again, my day's darling,
My little child who preferred the bright apple to gold,
And who lies with the shining world on his innocent eyes,
Though night-long I feel your tears, bright as the rose
In its sorrowful leaves, on my lips, and feel your hands
Touching my cheek, and wondering 'Are those your tears?'
O grief, that your heart should know the tears that seem empty
    years
And the worlds that are falling!

142

THE SOLDAN'S SONG

When green as a river was the barley,
Green as a river the rye,
I waded deep and began to parley
With a youth whom I heard sigh.
'I seek,' said he, 'a lovely lady,
A nymph as bright as a queen,
Like a tree that drips with pearls her shady
Locks of hair were seen;
And all the rivers became her flocks
Though their wool you cannot shear,
Because of the love of her flowing locks.
The kingly sun like a swain
Came strong, unheeding of her scorn,
Wading in deeps where she has lain,
Sleeping upon her river lawn
And chasing her starry satyr train.
She fled, and changed into a tree, —
That lovely fair-haired lady . . .
And now I seek through the sere summer
Where no trees are shady.'

HEART AND MIND

Said the Lion to the Lioness—'When you are amber dust,—
No more a raging fire like the heat of the Sun
(No liking but all lust)—
Remember still the flowering of the amber blood and bone
The rippling of bright muscles like a sea,
Remember the rose-prickles of bright paws
Though we shall mate no more
Till the fire of that sun the heart and the moon-cold bone are one.'

Said the Skeleton lying upon the sands of Time—
'The great gold planet that is the mourning heat of the Sun
Is greater than all gold, more powerful
Than the tawny body of a Lion that fire consumes
Like all that grows or leaps . . . . so is the heart
More powerful than all dust. Once I was Hercules
Or Samson, strong as the pillars of the seas:
But the flames of the heart consumed me, and the mind
Is but a foolish wind.'

Said the Sun to the Moon—'When you are but a lonely white
            crone,
And I, a dead King in my golden armour somewhere in a dark
            wood,
Remember only this of our hopeless love
That never till Time is done
Will the fire of the heart and the fire of the mind be one.'

144